Toiling Upward

Toiling Upward

The Lester Family of Henry County Virginia

By Thomas D. Perry

In Domine Gloria Mea "In God Our Glory"

ISBN-13: 978-1463787288
ISBN-10: 1463787286

Laurel Hill Publishing LLC
Thomas D. Perry
4443 Ararat Highway
P. O. Box 11
Ararat, VA 24053
276-692-5300
freestateofpatrick@yahoo.com
www.freestateofpatrick.com

Copyright 2011 Laurel Hill Publishing LLC

In memory of Parker Turner Lester and Lottie Shelton Lester.

"Daddy always said 'Cap'n Til' married two great ladies"
-- Ralph Clayton Lester

"We were blessed with two wonderful mothers."
--Julia Lester Oakley

Also by Thomas D. Perry

Ascent to Glory: The Genealogy of J. E. B. Stuart

The Free State of Patrick: Patrick County Virginia in the Civil War

J. E. B. Stuart's Birthplace: The History of the Laurel Hill Farm

Images of America: Patrick County Virginia

Images of America: Henry County Virginia

Then and Now: Patrick County Virginia

Notes from the Free State of Patrick:
Patrick County, Virginia, and Regional History

God's Will Be Done: The Christian Life of J. E. B. Stuart

Patrick County Oral History Project: A Guide

J. E. B. Stuart's Birthplace: A Guide for Educators and Visitors

Martinsville Virginia

Fieldale Virginia

Visit www.freestateofpatrick.com for more information

Table of Contents

Chapter One	Lester Branch	1
Chapter Two	Fighting with J. E. B. Stuart	7
Chapter Three	A Wayward Child	27
Chapter Four	Big Jane and Big Lucy	39
Chapter Five	All Roads Lead To Waidsboro	57
Chapter Six	Tobacco, Timber, and Parker	73
Chapter Seven	Finney Woods to Jones Creek	87
Chapter Eight	Living in a Wedding Cake	101
Chapter Nine	Swimming Pool and a Castle	109
Chapter Ten	Cap'n Til and Lottie	119
Chapter Eleven	Flying High	131
Chapter Twelve	Lottie's Children	139
Chapter Thirteen	Ralph	149
Chapter Fourteen	Lester Images	157
Conclusion	The Lesters of Henry County Virginia	185
Appendix	Virginia Legislative Resolution	187
	Patent for Plug Tobacco Machine	189
	Patent for Furnace	203
Acknowledgements		211
Bibliography		213

About Thomas D. Perry

J. E. B. Stuart's biographer Emory Thomas describes Tom Perry as "a fine and generous gentleman who grew up near Laurel Hill, where Stuart grew up, has founded J. E. B. Stuart Birthplace and attracted considerable interest in the preservation of Laurel Hill. He has started a symposium series about aspects of Stuart's life to sustain interest in Stuart beyond Ararat, Virginia." Perry holds a BA in History from Virginia Tech in 1983. Tom started the J. E. B. Stuart Birthplace Preservation Trust, Inc. in 1990. The non-profit organization preserved 75 acres of the Stuart property including the house site where James Ewell Brown Stuart was born on February 6, 1833. Perry wrote the eight interpretive signs about Laurel Hill's history along with the Virginia Civil War Trails sign and the new Virginia Historical Highway Marker in 2002. He spent many years researching traveling all over the nation to find Stuart materials including two trips across the Mississippi River to visit nearly every place "Jeb" Stuart served in the United States Army (1854-1861). He continues his work to preserve Stuart's Birthplace producing the Laurel Hill Teacher's Guide for educators and the Laurel Hill Reference Guide for groups and the organization to share his lifetime of research on the only preserved site in the nation relating to the birthplace and boyhood home of James Ewell Brown Stuart. Tom can be seen on Virginia Public Television's Forgotten Battlefields: The Civil War in Southwest Virginia with his mentor noted Civil War Historian Dr. James I. Robertson, Jr. Perry has begun a collection of papers relating to Stuart and Patrick County history in the Special Collections Department of the Carol M. Newman Library at Virginia Tech under the auspices of the Virginia Center For Civil War Studies. In 2004, Perry began the Free State Of Patrick Internet History Group, which has become the largest historical organization in the area with over 500 members. It covers Patrick County Virginia and regional history. Tom produces a monthly email newsletter about regional history entitled Notes from the Free State of Patrick that goes from his website www.freestateofpatrick.com.

"The heights by great men gained and kept,

Were not attained by sudden flight,

But , while their companions slept

Were Toiling upward in the night.

--Henry Wadsworth Longfellow

Chapter One

Lester Branch

Many thought the house looked like a "Wedding Cake." Others described it as a medieval fortress, but the white brick home on Starling Avenue in Martinsville, Virginia, was home for George W. Lester ll. As a boy he sat on the porch in the years just after World War Two listening to his father George Tilden "Cap'n Til" Lester swap stories about the past with his father-in-law Ferdinand Shelton. Young George remembered falling asleep on the porch as the stories of his family's past wafted over him like a wave of dreams taking him back in time.

The first Lester in Virginia was Thomas, age 32, living at James City (Jamestown) in February 1623. Twenty years later, Ralph Lester was living in James City in York County. Three years later Robert Lester was living in Virginia along with Thomas four years later. By 1776, twenty different families of Lesters lived in Virginia and North Carolina. Among these head of households were Alexander, Benjamin, Jeremiah, John, and William. A Benjamin Lester served as one of the personal body guards known as "Commander in Chief Guards" to George Washington in 1777 during the American Revolution. In 1782, a William Lester, the son of Thomas Lester, was living in Pittsylvania County.

Thomas H. Lester (1730-1788) married Sytha (last name unknown) in 1750. Thomas H. Lester was executor of his brother William's will on January 26, 1776, in Halifax County. His son John (1780-1873) married first Nancy Collins (1785-1815) in 1800. This union produced three sons Thomas, Jesse, and William A. and two daughters Polly Lester Stultz and Nancy Lester Haley. After Nancy's death, John Lester married for the second time in 1815 to Anna Minter (1792-1886). Their sons were Daniel, Benjamin, James, and Jeremiah. Daughters of John and Anna were Eliza Lester Haley and Susan Jane Lester Richardson. John, born in Pittsylvania County, served in the Virginia Militia during the War of 1812.

Elected Constable in Martinsville in 1841, Daniel Lester moved to South Carolina in 1853. He served in Company C, 2nd Battalion South Carolina Infantry. After the Civil War, he moved to Jackson County, North Carolina. His land is now under the waters behind Fontana Dam in western North Carolina.

John Lester moved to the Lester Branch of Beaver Creek in Henry County, Virginia, by 1823. The county formed in 1776 from Pittsylvania County while Franklin County to the north formed in 1786 from Bedford and Henry Counties. The first record of the Lesters in Henry County was on September 8, 1823, in Deed Book 10, page 9, when William Parsley and John Davis through their attorney Moses Pedigo sold John Lester of Pittsylvania County 269 acres of land on Beaver Creek for $294. There are no records of the Lesters in Franklin County to the north until 1871. The following year the Lesters joined the Leatherwood Primitive Baptist Church. Jeremiah and Benjamin were to receive John Lester's home place on the Lester Branch of Beaver Creek, but Henry Clay Lester acquired the property to pay off debts owned by Jeremiah.

In 1840, many Lesters are living in Henry County included Thomas, Daniel, William and John. William had sons under the age of five and one age 5-10 years old. John had one under age five and two sons between 5-10 years of age along with one 15-20. The census lists the African-American slaves of the family for the first time as "Aliens" in a separate category. Thomas owned one female, while William and John owned three females each.

The 1850 United States Census lists John Lester living in Henry County at age 70 with his wife Ann age 58, Benjamin age 19 and others. Thomas Lester is listed nearby at age 49 with wife Frances age 36, Dorothy age 17, Thomas H., William and Jesse.

John Lester's son William A. Lester, Sr. married Frances H. Stegall on November 20, 1832. The 1850 Census reported William Ainsley Lester age 47 living in Henry County with his wife Frances Stegall Lester, age 41 with children including

William Jr. age 15, George age 14, Henry age 12, Julia age 10, John age 7, Marshall age 5 and Sarah age 1. The 1850 Census lists William A. Lester's worth at $159 including one female slave age 15.

In 1860, the Census of Henry County shows William Ainsley Lester Sr. age 57, living as a farmer in the Dyer's Store section with real estate valued at $2,800 and personal property valued at $2,500. His wife Frances, age 51, lived with her husband and children William Jr. age 26, George Washington age 24, Henry Clay age 22, John age 18, Marshall age 15, Sarah age 10 and Susan age 6. The census lists William, George, and Henry Clay Lester as "Tobcconist" in the census. John and Anna Lester are living next to William and Frances. The neighbors of the Lesters included William Pedigo and Daniel Pace along with Washington Flood age 50, who had real estate valued at $10,000 and personal property valued at $30,000. This information is what we know about the Lesters before War Between the States while living on Lester Branch.

William A. Lester Agricultural Census	1850	1860
Acres Improved	50	100
Acres Unimproved	203	140
Cash Value of Acreage	$759	$2800
Cash Value of Farm Implements	$20	$50
Horses	1	4
Milk Cows	3	2
Ox	0	1
Cattle	3	6
Sheep	25	20
Swine	18	25
Value of Livestock	$203	?
Wheat (in bushels)	40	80
Corn	275	275
Oats	72	15
Peas	0	2
Potatoes	10	20
Sweet Potatoes	30	30
Butter (in pounds)	156	125
Wool	30	6
Bees Wax/Honey	75	100
Value of Homemade Manufacturing	$49	$35
Value of Animals Slaughtered	$74	$92
Tobacco (in pounds)	2300	3800

Chapter Two
Fighting With J. E. B. Stuart

The history of the tenth regiment of cavalry from the Commonwealth of Virginia began early in the war with former Governor and Brigadier General Henry Wise, one of those political generals that often become a disaster during any war. He led the Wise Legion, whose official title was the 46th Virginia Infantry Regiment that included a regiment of cavalry that became the tenth regiment. These mounted men came from colorfully named units such as the Caskie Mounted Rangers, Henrico Light Dragoons, Rosser's Mounted Rangers, and other units from Rockbridge and Albemarle counties.

In 1862, the regiment left the Wise Legion on May 25, 1862, and for a short time was the Eighth Virginia Cavalry Battalion, but officially became the Tenth Virginia Cavalry with the following companies. Companies A, Caskie's Mounted Rangers, known also as Fry's Mounted Rangers, made up of men from Richmond. The unit was originally Company C, First Cavalry, Wise Virginia Legion. Company B, the Carolina Rangers from Davie County, present day Mocksville, North Carolina, were originally Company H, First Cavalry, Wise Virginia Legion. Company C, Captain William W. Flood's Company included the

Lesters organized on March 20, 1862. Company D, Wise Mounted Guard organized in Richmond in April 2, 1862. They were originally Company I, First Cavalry, Wise Virginia Legion. This unit served temporarily in September 1862 as Company C, 32nd Virginia Cavalry Battalion. The first Company E, Jennings Wise Hussars organized on May 13, 1862, in Richmond with men from Louisiana and other states. This unit disbanded on February 8, 1864, and the men joined other units. The second Company E organized on April 7, 1864, with men from Company A, 12th North Carolina Cavalry Battalion and Company H, Dearing's Confederate States Cavalry Regiment. Company F, the Albemarle Rangers were once Company F, First Cavalry, Wise Virginia Cavalry Legion. Company G, the Jackson Rangers originated as Company E, First Cavalry, Wise Virginia Legion. Company H, the Valley Rangers, also known as the Rockingham Cavalry. This unit originally called Company D, Wise Virginia Legion hailed from Rockingham County, Virginia. Company I, the Henrico Light Dragoons, was originally Company A, First Cavalry, Wise Virginia Legion. Company K, the Texas Rangers, started originally as Rosser's Mounted Rangers and the Virginia Mounted Rangers were Company H, First Cavalry, Wise Virginia Legion. Others called the Tenth Virginia Cavalry by its commander's names throughout the war as J. Lucius Davis' Cavalry, Robert A.

Caskie's Cavalry, and others such as Zachariah S. McGruder, William B. Clement, Joseph T. Rosser, Louis J. Hawley, Edgar S. Phelps, William L. Graham, William E. Hinton, and James W. Timberlake.

George Washington Lester I enlisted at Shady Grove in southern Franklin County on February 28, 1862, just north of his Henry County home. His unit was Company C under the command of Captain William Washington Flood came into the regiment after mustering together at Shady Grove. Flood, born in 1837, enlisted on March 4, 1862, at Franklin Court House. He resigned on August 10, 1863, due to health reasons specifically "hemoraging from lungs." Flood died in Fort Worth, Texas, before 1921. The regiment under the command of Colonel J. L. Davis, Lt. Colonel Zachariah S. McGruder and Major Joseph Travis Rosser received assignment to the Cavalry Division under the command of Brigadier General, soon to be Major General, "Jeb" Stuart in the Army of Northern Virginia.

James Lucius Davis commanded the 10th Virginia Cavalry. Born in Clarke County, Virginia, on January 25, 1816, Davis graduated from the United States Military Academy at West Point, New York, in 1836. Davis continued a military career with interludes for farming in the Virginia. First, he fought in the war with the Creek Indians, and then returned to the Shenandoah

Valley of Virginia to farm. Next, Davis served as a Texas Ranger 1839-41 before returning to Virginia to farm in Henrico County near Richmond where the 1860 Census found him just before the outbreak of the War Between the States. He served on the staff of Brigadier General Henry Wise before receiving assignment to the Tenth Virginia Cavalry on August 13, 1861.

Lieutenant Colonel Zachariah S. McGruder was 31 years old at the beginning of the war. Hailing from Henrico County, he served in the Virginia House of Delegates. He resigned in September 1863 due to ill health, but recovered quickly to become a member of the Virginia General Assembly. He survived the war became a physician and lived on until 1896.

Major Joseph Travis Rosser was a forty-year-old lawyer and graduate of the University of Virginia when the war broke out. He served as a Collector of Customs in Petersburg and a three-year stint as U. S. Attorney in present day Minnesota before he enlisted in June 1861 in Richmond. At Brandy Station on June 9, 1863, he commanded the 10th Virginia Regiment during the latter part of the battle. He resigned from his commission on August 8, 1863, and worked in the military courts, Conscript Bureau (The Confederate States of America had the first draft in U. S. History.) and Treasury Department before the end of the war.

In the summer of 1862, the 10th Virginia Cavalry did not participate in J. E. B. Stuart's "First Ride Around McClellan," where Stuart took 1,200 men on a complete circumference of the hundred thousand man Union Army of the Potomac losing only one man and giving Robert E. Lee's valuable information as to the placement of the "Yankees." Instead G. W. Lester and his compatriots found themselves in a picket line from the James River to Charles City Court House before falling back to Richmond before the Battles of Seven Days. Some of the men were not impressed with their 29-year-old commander from Patrick County. One member of Company F wrote his mother, "We can't go to town and only two mile from it. I despise to be under Genl. Steward he has no feeling. Cares nothing for the comfort of his men."

As Stuart moved to meet Thomas J. "Stonewall" Jackson, who was coming from the Shenandoah Valley, the Tenth found itself along the Nine Mile Road near R. E. Lee's headquarters. As the Seven Days Battles erupted around Richmond with Lee trying to push Union General George B. McClellan from the outskirts of the Confederate Capitol, the men of the Tenth found itself under fire of Union gunboats at Curl's Neck on the James River. After the fighting, the regiment moved twelve then twenty-five miles south of Richmond keeping an eye on the forces of the United States.

J. E. B. Stuart reorganized his cavalry division. The 10th Virginia was now part of the brigade of the South Carolinian Wade Hampton with the 1st North Carolina Cavalry, Cobb's Legions of Georgia, and the Jeff Davis Legion of Mississippi. Hampton, a wealthy civilian, was one of two men to go from private to Lieutenant General in the service of the Confederate States of America. The other was the formidable Nathan Bedford Forrest. Hampton eventually succeeded Stuart after the latter's death in 1864.

With McClellan bottled up at Harrison's Landing along the James River, the regiment eventually went from picket duty to a camp of instruction near Hanover Court House. Stuart was big on training his men. While Southerners grew up in the saddle, riding a horse, and fighting in a regiment of cavalry were not the same thing. Stuart's men viewed this sort of instruction as drudgery at the time, but later they came to the see the value that this sort of training had in making them a cohesive fighting force under Stuart.

Robert E. Lee moved his Army of Northern Virginia north in the summer of 1862 marching them into the history books as one of the greatest armies of all time. Fighting at Cedar Mountain, Second Manassas and eventually along the banks of Antietam

Creek near Sharpsburg, Maryland, with Jackson and James Longstreet commanding the infantry corps and Stuart, the cavalry division. Lee rode the Confederate wave to the outskirts of Washington that nearly ended the war that summer.

After Antietam, Stuart made his "Second Ride Around McClellan" also known as the Chambersburg Raid. Major Rosser took 150 men of the 10th Virginia on this raid. On November 10, 1862, Stuart reorganized his cavalry again with the 10th Virginia became part of the W. H. F. "Rooney" Lee's Brigade including the 5th, 9th, 15th Virginia regiments and 2nd North Carolina. The 13th Virginia replaced the 5th Virginia. William Henry Fitzhugh Lee, General Robert E. Lee's youngest son was a graduate of Harvard University and a large man described by a contemporary as "Too big to be a man, but too small to be a horse."

Born on May 31, 1837, to Robert Edward and Mary Custis Lee, William Henry Fitzhugh Lee was the second son born at Arlington House, now Arlington National Cemetery. He attended Harvard before joining the U. S. Army in 1857. Two years later he was living at the White House Plantation along the Pamunkey River, south of Richmond, where reportedly George Washington courted Martha Custis. Mary Custis Lee was the granddaughter from the first marriage of Martha before she married the "Father" of our country. W. H. F. "Rooney" Lee rose from Captain in the

Confederate Cavalry before becoming Colonel of the 9th Virginia Cavalry. The new brigade marched to Fredericksburg on November 18. Eleven days later the regiment was at Guinea's Station along the Richmond, Fredericksburg, and Potomac Railroad needing forage for their horses. On December 4, 1862, the regiment saw Confederate Artillery battle Union gunboats near Port Royal in the Rappahannock River.

After the horrendous battle of Fredericksburg, the regiment went into winter quarters at Guinea Station then moved to Essex and then King and Queen County along the Northern Neck of Virginia. As spring began to bloom, the regiment returned to guarding the fords along the Rappahannock River near Fredericksburg. In April one of the men reported, "Our army is better now than it ever was before, well drilled and well disciplined, fine spirits and in fine health anxious for a fight."

The regiment did not have long to wait. Union General George Stoneman, commanding the cavalry of Union General Joseph Hooker, led a raid towards Richmond. "Rooney" Lee, now a Brigadier General, took his brigade minus the 10th Virginia to pursue Stoneman. Hooker replaced Ambrose Burnside, who fought the hapless battle at Fredericksburg. Burnside replaced McClellan, who replaced John Pope after the latter lost to Lee at Second Manassas. Lincoln replaced McClellan after he retreated from the outskirts of Richmond during the Seven Days Battles. John Pope next commanded the Union Army of the Potomac. President Abraham Lincoln continued to find commanders to lead his Army of the Potomac until June 1863, when George Gordon Meade became the final commander of the army.

In May 1863, Stuart moved his cavalry to Culpeper County near a station on the Orange and Alexandria Railroad called Brandy Station. On May 22, Stuart held the first of three reviews of his troopers at Auburn, the home of pro-Union sympathizer John Minor Botts. On May 25, the 10th Virginia had 27 officers and 259 men ready for duty with one officer and 72 men present, but not effective. There were 16 officers and 345 men absent on other duty. Among these was George Washington Lester I.

On May 31, one of the men wrote, "We are living better than we have for some time." Stuart again reviewed his troops on June 5 and three days later on June 8. Stuart used these pageants to inspire "spirit" in his men.

James Ewell Brown "Jeb" Stuart was born in Ararat, Patrick County, Virginia, on February 6, 1833, to Archibald and Elizabeth Letcher Pannill Stuart. His uncle, William Letcher Pannill's family made their own mark on Martinsville and Henry County in the 1900s with Pannill Knitting Company. Stuart spent his first twelve years in "The Free State Of Patrick" before going to Wytheville for school for three years, then two years at Emory and Henry College before graduating from the United States Military Academy at West Point, New York, in 1854. Stuart served seven years in the U. S. Army, mainly in Kansas, before resigning in May 1861 to offer his sword to Virginia.

      June 8, 1863, was a day of pomp and pageantry. Robert E. Lee reviewed the cavalry of his army much to the pleasure of Stuart, his thirty-year-old cavalry commander. John Minor Botts's home Auburn was the site of the review. Bott, a Union sympathizer, was a favorite target of Stuart because of his pro-Union politics and the rolling hills of plantation near the railroad and the river. General Lee rode his famous mount Traveler around the cavalry with only "Jeb" Stuart able to keep up with his former West Point Superintendent. Lee first met Stuart in 1852 while the latter was student at the United States Military Academy where Lee was Superintendent. The relationship made the history books again in 1859 when Stuart accompanied Lee to Harper's Ferry to put down John Brown's attempt to take the United States Arsenal. Lee sent Stuart to firehouse where townspeople earlier trapped Brown and his raiders. Stuart confronted Brown, who he recognized from his time in the First U. S. Cavalry in Kansas. Stuart now in his second year commanding the cavalry and the end of his first year commanding Lee's cavalry, was near the zenith of his career. Stuart was at the height of his career with nearly 10,000 men mounted in his cavalry. One month earlier at the Battle of Chancellorsville, he replaced the wounded Thomas J. "Stonewall" Jackson as commander of the Second Corps on infantry in the Army of Northern Virginia and one month later he helped Lee get back from, Pennsylvania, into Virginia.

What George Washington Lester thought of all this is unknown, but no doubt he saw Generals Lee and Stuart on June 8, 1863, as he sat his new horse. Lester stood five foot nine inches tall with dark hair, dark eyes and a dark complexion accentuated by the constant time in the saddle under the blazing summer sun serving in Company C, 10th Virginia Cavalry.

G. W. Lester I returned home to Henry County in May and June of 1863 to get a new horse. Southern horsemen had to supply their own mounts while their northern counterparts received animals from "Honest Abe's" War Department. G. W. Lester remained with his regiment from July 1863 through August 1864.

George Washington Lester I had a new horse. It was June 9, 1863, and the 10th Virginia Cavalry was in Culpeper County, Virginia, along the Rappahannock River near a small country town called Brandy Station. The station along the Orange and Alexandria Railroad got its name from the local alcohol product. The Tenth Virginia Cavalry regiment served in the brigade of

Brigadier General W. H. F. "Rooney" Lee, the son of the commanding general of the Army of Northern Virginia Robert E. Lee, in the Cavalry Division of Major General James Ewell Brown "Jeb" Stuart. Stuart hailed from Ararat, Virginia, in Patrick County about sixty miles from Lester's home in northern Henry County.

On the morning of June 9, the Cavalry Corps of J. E. B. Stuart was to move north. Early that day the sound of gun fire and the sight of blue cavalry soon replaced the revelry of the review the previous day as Lester and his regiment found itself embroiled in one of the largest fights ever seen on horseback in the history of the entire Western Hemisphere. As Union General John Buford pushed against W. H. F. Lee's Brigade, the men in gray fell back to a "Stonewall" on the northern end of Fleetwood Hill. Later the regiment fell back south towards another part of the battle where Stuart's headquarters was the night before.

Described by one of his trooper as "here, there and everywhere," General Stuart felt the pressure of an attack from the cavalry of Union General Alfred Pleasanton on multiple fronts. One trooper of the 10th Virginia described the Battle of Brandy Station as "the hardest cavalry fight we have had since the war began." With W. H. F. Lee wounded, Colonel Solomon Williams of the 2nd North Carolina took command of the brigade and quickly lost his life. Colonel Davis of the 10th took command of the brigade leaving Major Rosser in command of the regiment. John Chambliss, senior commander on the field took command of the brigade later in the day. One member of the regiment estimated 70 killed or wounded with another 50 captured.

During the course of the battle George Washington Lester lost his new horse. Dismounted, he found himself coming face to face with a red headed Ohioan, who was not interested in accepting Lester's surrender. George later told his family he had no choice, but to shoot and kill the "Yankee" as the Battle of Brandy Station raged all around him. This was the only man he knowingly killed during the course of the entire war.

Wounded at Brandy Station, Union forces captured W. H. F. Lee on June 26 at his wife, Charlotte Wickham's ancestral home, Hickory Hill, near Richmond. A POW in New York and exchanged on February 25, 1864, Lee surrendered as a Major General. He married Mary T. Bolling in 1867. He served in the Virginia Senate for three years beginning in 1875. After serving in the United States House of Representatives in 1887, Lee died in 1891 at his home Ravensworth.

The 10th Virginia Cavalry Regiment continued with Stuart on the controversial ride to a Pennsylvania town named Gettysburg. On July 3, the regiment fought against George Custer and David M. Gregg in the massive cavalry fight east of Gettysburg.

Union forces captured Colonel J. Lucius on July 6, 1863, during the withdrawal from Gettysburg after wounding him near Frederick, Maryland. Davis spent a month in the hospital with aliments including a sprained ankle before receiving a transfer to Patterson Park Hospital in Baltimore with a "contusion." Davis eventually made his way as a prisoner of war to Fort McHenry where Frances Scott Key wrote the national anthem "The Star Spangled Banner" during the War of 1812. Davis then went to prisons at Johnson's Island on Lake Erie and Point Lookout, Maryland. Davis returned to Confederate command leading a brigade near Petersburg, Virginia, in August 1864.

Robert Alexander Caskie received promotion to Major on August 8, 1863, and quickly to Lieutenant Colonel on September 11. Caskie, born in Richmond in 1830, attended the University of Virginia from 1850-51. Listed as a "Tobacco Merchant" in the 1860 Census in Richmond, Caskie enlisted in Company A on June 9, 1861. On June 12, 1864, General Chambliss applied for Caskie's promotion to Colonel stating, "Col. Caskie is in every respect qualified for the position, has commanded the Regiment for nearly a year and has brought it to a high state of efficiency." Caskie received a wound in the leg at Reams Station on August 23, 1864, but returned by the end of November. He was in a hospital at the end of March 1865, but surrendered at Appomattox after finally receiving his promotion to Colonel. He worked in Richmond and in Missouri as a tobacco merchant before he died in Merion, Pennsylvania, on August 31, 1928. His mortal remains lie in Richmond's Hollywood Cemetery with his commanding officer J. E. B. Stuart.

Gettysburg Campaign Army of Northern Virginia Cavalry Division

Major General James E. B. Stuart

Hampton's Brigade- Brig. General Wade Hampton; Colonel Laurence S. Baker

1st North Carolina Cavalry- Col. Laurence S. Baker

1st South Carolina Cavalry- Col. John L. Black

2nd South Carolina Cavalry- Col. Matthew C. Butler

Cobb's (Georgia) Legion- Col. Pierce B. L. Young

Jeff Davis (Mississippi) Legion- Col. Joseph F. Waring

Phillips' (Georgia) Legion- Lt. Col. Jefferson C. Phillips

Fitz Lee's Brigade- Brig. General W. Fitzhugh Lee

1st Virginia Cavalry- Col. James H. Drake

2nd Virginia Cavalry- Col. Thomas T. Munford

3rd Virginia Cavalry- Col. Thomas H. Owen

4th Virginia Cavalry- Col. William Carter Wickham

1st Maryland Battalion- Maj. Harry Gilmore; Maj. Ridgely Brown

Robertson's Brigade- Brig. General Beverly H. Robertson

4th North Carolina Cavalry- Col. Dennis D. Ferebee

5th North Carolina Cavalry- Col. Peter G. Evans

Jones's Brigade- Brig. General William E. Jones

6th Virginia Cavalry- Maj. Cabel E. Flourney

7th Virginia Cavalry- Lt. Col. Thomas Marshall

11th Virginia Cavalry- Col. Lunsford L. Lomax

W. H. F. Lee's Brigade- Colonel John R. Chambliss, Jr.

2nd North Carolina Cavalry- Lt. Col. William Payne; Capt. Walter A. Graham; Lt. Joseph Baker

9th Virginia Cavalry- Col. Richard L. T. Beale

10th Virginia Cavalry- Col. J. Lucius Davis

13th Virginia Cavalry- Capt. Benjamin F. Winfield

Stuart's Horse Artillery- Major Robert F. Beckham

Breathed's (Virginia) Battery- Capt. James Breathed

Chew's (Virginia) Battery- Capt. R. Preston Chew

Griffin's (Maryland) Battery- Capt. William H. Griffin

Hart's (South Carolina) Battery- Capt. James F. Hart

McGregor's (Virginia) Battery- Capt. William M. McGregor

Moorman's (Virginia) Battery- Capt. Marcellus M. Moorman

Jenkins' Brigade- Brig. General Albert G. Jenkins; Colonel Milton J. Ferguson

14th Virginia Cavalry- Maj. Benjamin F. Eakle

16th Virginia Cavalry- Col. Milton J. Ferguson

17th Virginia Cavalry- Col. William H. French

34th Virginia Battalion- Lt. Col. Vincent A. Witcher

36th Virginia Battalion- Capt. Cornelius T. Smith

Jackson's (Virginia) Battery- Capt. Thomas E. Jackson

Imboden's Command- Brig. General John D. Imboden

18th Virginia Cavalry- Col. George W. Imboden

62nd Virginia Infantry, Mounted- Col. George H. Smith

Virginia Partisan Rangers- Capt. John H. McNeill

Virginia (Staunton) Battery- Capt. John H. McClanahan

The Quartermaster caught up with the regiment in September 1863 bringing sorely needed shoes, pants, jackets, shirts, drawers, socks, caps, and tent flys to the men. George continued on receiving clothing in October and December 1864. The 2nd North Carolina left the brigade leaving the 9th, 10th, and 13th Virginia together for the rest of the war.

That fall of 1863, the regiment guarded the Rappahannock at Raccoon and Morton fords. More fighting came in October, being part of the "Buckland Races," where Stuart laid a trap for the Union cavalry that obligingly fell for. In November, the last review of the cavalry at the Botts Farm in Culpeper County occurred. The regiment found itself in the Shenandoah Valley in December going as far south as Fincastle just north of Roanoke. Christmas was at Staunton and New Years at New Market, Virginia.

In March 1864, Company C of the 10th Virginia had 62 men present for duty. April found them in Madison County and on May 9, the regiment found itself on Robert E. Lee's right flank at Spotsylvania Court House, where Lee and the new commander of the Union Armies U. S. Grant locked in mortal combat for the future of the country.

Jeremiah Lester served in the 10th Virginia Cavalry as a private in Company C enlisting the same day as his cousin George Washington Lester on February 25, 1862. Desertion marred his service in April 1863 with a listing of "Absent Without Leave." While many soldiers of the Confederate States of America went AWOL, Jeremiah's case was different. Imprisoned by Confederate authorities beginning in December 1863 until April 1864 in Castle Thunder Prison in Richmond, Jeremiah volunteered to defend Richmond during Union General Philip Sheridan's May 1864 raid on Richmond as a member of Winder's Legion. Jeremiah received a pardon from a death sentence by President Jefferson Davis. J. E. B. Stuart lost his life on May 12, 1864, after one of George Custer's men shot him the day before just north of Richmond at a crossroads called Yellow Tavern as part of Sheridan's raid.

With the death of Patrick County's J. E. B. Stuart, joint command of the Cavalry Corps went to Wade Hampton and Fitzhugh Lee. Robert E. Lee appointed Hampton to command of the cavalry and the war went on for another eleven months that were memorable for Henry County's George W. Lester I.

Chapter Three
A Wayward Child

In May 1864, John R. Chambliss commanded the brigade that included the 10th Virginia Cavalry. Chambliss hailed from Greensville County, Virginia, and graduated from the USMA at West Point, New York in 1853, one of fifteen Civil War Generals including John Bell Hood in that class. A lawyer and politician before the war, Chambliss, born a week before J. E. B. Stuart, in January 1833, served in the U. S. Army including a tour teaching at the cavalry school at Carlisle Barracks before returning home to Hicksville, Virginia. Chambliss lost his life in August 1864 on the Charles City Road near Richmond. R. E. Lee said of him, "the loss sustained by the cavalry in the fall of General Chambliss will be felt throughout the army, in which, by his courage, energy, and skill, he had won for himself an honorable name."

The 10th Virginia fought at Haw's Shop on May 27, 1864, and Reams Station along the Welden Railroad on August 25. In November, Lester's Company C had 78 men present of these 62 were mounted. Near Belfield, the regiment received ten new uniforms, shoes, and tents. Among the men of the regiment was Thomas G. Penn of Patrick County, now part of Company G. Penn's family became part of the American Tobacco Company and Aurora "The Pink House," the large house in Patrick County that is on the Virginia and National Registers of Historic Places was their home.

George Washington Lester I siblings included William Ainsley Lester, Jr. born at Dyer's Store on September 8, 1835. He died on April 7, 1905, at Figsboro, in Henry County. Known as "Cap'n Bill," he served in Company K of the 57th Virginia Infantry Regiment enlisting on July 10, 1861. He received promotion to Sergeant on December 10, 1861, and then to Lieutenant on May 7, 1862. He was present through December before resigning on January 3, 1863.

John J. Allen organized Company K, the "Botetourt Guards" of the 57th Virginia Infantry Regiment. Lewis Armistead was the first colonel of the regiment and later led the brigade the regiment served. John Bowie Magruder replaced Armistead as colonel of the regiment. They fought in the horrendous charge of the Army of Northern Virginia made on July 1, 1862, at Malvern Hill during the Seven Days Battles outside Richmond. They marched to the field on the Long Bridge Road and completed two charges after 6 p.m. on the Confederate right flank. The regiment was at the Battle of Sharpsburg along Antietam Creek in September 1862. Three months later the regiment was present at Fredericksburg, but saw no action. After W. A. Lester left the unit the 57th Virginia fought in Pickett's Charge on the third day of Gettysburg, where Armistead lost his life.

John Carlton Lester (1843-1898) served in 57th Virginia Infantry before marrying Julia Frances. He enlisted on July 10, 1861, and was present through June 1863. Wounded at Gettysburg, he received promotion to Sergeant in October 1864. Captured at Five Forks, Virginia, on April 1, 1865, John spent two months at Hart's Island, New York, before taking the oath of allegiance and returning home. He stood 5 foot nine and one half inches tall with fair complexion, light hair, and brown eyes.

In June 1864, William Ainsley Lester Jr. found himself a part of history. He was one of the first Americans conscripted or drafted into military service by the Confederate States of America. On the 19th, William was at Camp Lee. On June 21, 1864, he was with his brother George assigned to the 10th Virginia Cavalry as a Private in Company C. He received clothes in October and December 1864. He stood five foot ten inches tall with a light complexion, dark brown hair, and eyes.

In January 1865, George Washington Lester was again absent from the 10th Virginia Cavalry. During this time a trip home to secure another horse was probably the cause. During this visit a conversation with his mother about the cause of Southern Independence possibly occurred. The story is that George told his mother Frances Stegall Lester that she should sell her slaves because the South was going to lose the war. He told her he was going to sell "his Reuben" while he was home. Her response to her son was that if they lost, she did not want to see him again. "Get your horse and get back to the battlefield. If the South loses, I do not wish to lay eyes on you again!"

Often stories passed down orally are hard to verify, but in this case George Washington Lester owned an African-American male slave, age 38, in 1860. This is very likely the Reuben passed down in stories from the Civil War. William Lester owned three female slaves age 22, 8, and 6. Ten years earlier in 1850, William owned one female slave age 15. In 1860, the Lester's neighbor, Washington Flood owned thirty-five slaves ages 13-70.

In early 1865, the regimental flag of the 10th Virginia met an "inglorious end in the mouth of any army mule," but soon the Confederate government replaced it. George W. Lester I returned to the army soon enough to be captured on April 2-3, 1865, in Dinwiddie County, Virginia. As Robert E. Lee evacuated Richmond and Petersburg, Lester was on his way to prison at Point Lookout, Maryland. On April 13, George was at City Point, Virginia. Union forces also captured William A. Lester, Jr. at Ford's Depot on April 3, 1865.

Some members of the regiment continued on fighting at High Bridge on the Appomattox River and participating in the "last charge of the war" on April 9 at Appomattox Court House. One of the last men to die in the war was Corporal John Clodfelter of Company B and only two men from Lester's Company C surrendered on April 12, 1865. Many of the men of the regiment escaped with Fitzhugh Lee.

Point Lookout, Maryland, is in St. Mary's County, where the Potomac River empties into the Chesapeake Bay. As early as 1612, Captain John Smith explored the area. By 1830, the United States established a lighthouse on the spot. In 1862, federal authorities built Hammond Hospital at the tip of the point with wards rotating around a central hospital bay like spokes in a wheel for wounded and sick soldiers. After the Battle of Gettysburg in 1863, Confederate prisoners began to arrive. The camp's capacity was 10,000, but soon twice that numbers found themselves imprisoned. Over the next two years, 50,000 came through the camp with 3,384 buried there today. Estimates range from 4 to 14 thousand deaths at the camp. It is no doubt that living outside only in tents in the blazing heat to bone chilling cold along with polluted water, inadequate food, clothing and lack of medical attention led to the deaths of so many. Point Lookout was the largest Union prison camp with water on three sides and the guns of Fort Lincoln pointing at the prisoners. Only fifty escaped in two years. Another indignity placed on the Confederate prisoners was the United States Colored Troops acting as guards for their former owners. There is little doubt that at Point Lookout "bottom rail" was on top.

George Washington Lester I remained a prisoner of the United States until June 14, 1865. Paroled after swearing allegiance to the United States of America, he returned to Henry County "completely broke" with holes in his pants. His Company C of the Tenth Virginia Cavalry had 159 serve out of 2, 136 in the regiment. During the war 9 were discharged, 16 deserted, 11 died of disease, and 7 transferred.

After the war, Abram D. Reynolds, brother of R. J. Reynolds, like many other returning soldiers, made his mark on the world of business. His son started the Reynolds Metals Company, makers of products such as Reynolds Wrap. Reynolds had left Rock Spring Farm, the Reynolds Homestead operated today by Virginia Tech under the stigma of possibly causing the death of three of his siblings in October 1862 when he brought home cotton tainted with smallpox. He did not know what kind of reception he would receive upon arriving in Patrick County. He wrote years later: "My father was a fine disciplinarian and always kept me at a distance and I never knew he loved me until then when he saw me he ran to meet me and threw his arms around me and said 'My Son the Yankees have been here and torn up everything and my Negro men have all gone with them but since you have come back alive and well it is all right. We can rebuild our lost fortune.' I was glad my father made this demonstration it made a better man of me. Love is the greatest gift that was bestowed on man. It has brought back many wayward children. Parents should never give up on a wayward child."

One trend in the family lore is that the "famous Lester temper" came from the Stegall's and no doubt Frances Stegall Lester reconsidered her opinion with the bleak future the South had she needed every one of her sons home and safe. George Washington Lester I came home and picked up the pieces of his life and that of his beloved Virginia. He and his family continued to toil upward. Five years later in 1870 the census listed George Washington Lester living in Henry County, Virginia.

Assignments of the 10th Virginia Cavalry
May 17, 1862, Cavalry, Department of Norfolk.
May 28, 1862, Cavalry Brigade, Army of Northern Virginia.
July 28, 1862, First Brigade, Cavalry, Army of Northern Virginia.
March 14, 1863, Company D transferred to Department of Richmond.
September 20, 1862, Wade Hampton's Brigade, Cavalry Division, Army of Northern Virginia.
November 10, 1862, W. H. F. "Rooney" Lee's Brigade, Cavalry Division, Army of Northern Virginia.
December 10, 1862, Third Brigade, Cavalry Division, Army of Northern Virginia.
May 25, 1863, W. H. F. Lee's Brigade, Second Division, Cavalry Corps, Army of Northern Virginia.
September 9, 1863, W. H. F. Lee's Brigade, Fitzhugh Lee's Division, Cavalry Corps, Army of Northern Virginia.
May 1, 1864, Chambliss Brigade, W. H. F. Lee's Division, Cavalry Corps, Army of Northern Virginia.

George Washington Lester and Victoria Waid Lester

35

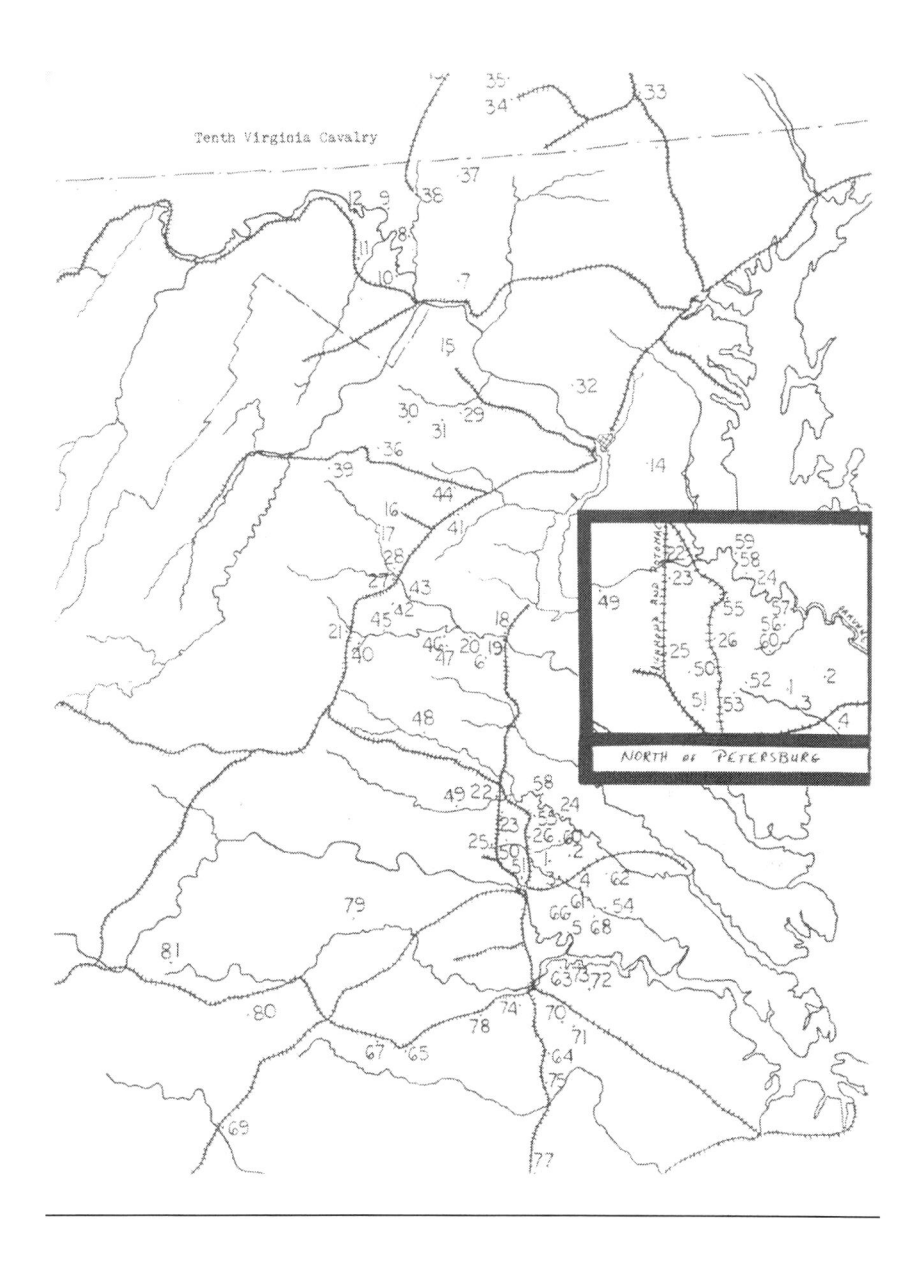

Engagements and Battles of the 10th Virginia Cavalry

(Numbers on left correspond to map on page 35)

June 25-July 1, 1862, Seven Days Battles
    1 Gaines Mill (June 27)
    2 Cold Harbor (June 27)
    3 Chickahominy (June 27)
    4 Bottom's Bridge (June 28-29)
    Skirmish at Fort Furnace (July 1)
5 Malvern Hill (August 5)
6 Thornburg/Massaponnax Church (August 5-6)
7 Skirmish at Catoctin Mountain, Maryland (September 13)
8 Battle of Antietam/Sharpsburg, Maryland (September 16-17)
9 Skirmish at Williamsport, Maryland (September 19-20)
10 Skirmish at Shepherdstown, West Virginia (October 1)
11 Martinsburg, West Virginia (October 1)
October 10-12, 1862, Stuart's Pennsylvania Raid
12 McCoy's Farm/Kinsell's Ferry, Maryland (October 10)
13 Chambersburg, Pennsylvania (October 10)
14 Fairview Heights, Maryland (October 10)
15 October 26-November 10, 1862, Operations in Loudon, Fauquier and Rappahannock Counties
16-17 Warrenton/Sulphur Springs, Virginia (November 15)
18 Falmouth, Virginia, (November 17)
19 December 12-15, Battle of Fredericksburg, Virginia
Rappahannock River (February 21, 1863)
20 April 27-May 6, Battle of Chancellorsville
April 29-May 8, Stoneman's Richmond Raid
21 Rapidan Station (May 1)
22 South Anna Bridge (May 3)
23 Ashland, Virginia (May 3)
24 Hanovertown Ferry, Virginia (May 4)
25 Hungry Station, Virginia (May 4)
26 Aylett's Virginia (May 5)
Grove Church, Virginia (May 8)
June 3-August 1, 1863, Gettysburg Campaign
27-28 Brandy Station (Fleetwood)/Beverly's Ford (June 9)

29 Aldie, Virginia (June 17-18)
30 Upperville, Virginia (June 21)
31 Middleburg, Virginia (June 21)
32 Rockville, Maryland (June 28)
33 Hanover, Pennsylvania (June 30)
34 Gettysburg, Pennsylvania (July 1-3)
35 Hunterstown, Pennsylvania (July 2)
36 Withdrawal to Manassas Gap, Virginia (July 5-24)
Skirmish at Green Oak, Pennsylvania (July 5)
37 Smithsburg, Maryland (July 5)
38 Hagerstown, Maryland (July 6)
 9 Williamsport, Maryland (July 6)
(Remainder of engagements are in Virginia)
39 Chester's Gap, Virginia (July 21-22)
27 Brandy Station (September 13)
21 Rapidan Station, Virginia (September 13-14)
40 Raccoon Ford, Rapidan Station (September 14-16)
41 Bristoe Station Campaign (October 9-22)
27 Brandy Station, Virginia (October 11)
42-43 Stevensburg/Kelly's Ford, Virginia (October 11)
16-17 Warrenton/White Sulphur Springs (October 12)
27 Brandy Station (October 12)
44 Buckland's Mills (October 19)
43 Kelly's Ford (November 7)
45 Mine Run Campaign (November 26- December 2, 1863)
Wilderness Campaign (May 4- June 12, 1864)
46 Battle of the Wilderness (May 5-7)
47 Todd's Tavern (May 7-8)
Sheridan's Raid To Richmond (May 9-24)
48 Davenport Ford, North Anna River (May 10)
49 Ground Squirrel Church (May 11)
22 South Anna River (May 11)
50 Yellow Tavern (May 11)
51 Brook's Church (May 12)
52 Mechanicsville (May 12)
53 Strawberry Hill (May 12)
 3 Meadow Bridge (May 12)
54 Jones Bridge (May 17)

55 Hanover Court House (May 21)
56 Haw's Shop (May 24)
57 Hanovertown (May 26)
60 Operations along the Totopotomoy River, Virginia (May 28-31)
56 Haw's Shop (June 3)
61 Long Bridge (June 12)
62 Smith's Store near St. Peter's Church (June 15)
63 Siege of Richmond and Petersburg (June 16, 1864-April 2, 1865)
64 Ream's Station, Virginia (June 22, 1864)
Operations against Wilson's Raid/Southside and Danville Railroad/Staunton River Bridge (June 22-July 2)
65 Black and White Station (June 23)
66 Charles City Court House (June 23)
67 Nottoway Court House (June 23)
68 New Market Heights/St. Mary's Church (June 24)
69 Staunton River Bridge (June 24-25)
64 Ream's Station (June 30-July 2, 1864)
70 Warwick Swamp (July 12)
71 Lee's Mills (July 12)
64 Ream's Station (July 12 and July 22)
72 Sycamore Church (September 16)
73 Coggin's Point (September 16)
Arthur's Swamp (September 30-October 1, 1864)
74 Boydton Plank Road/Hatcher's Run (October 27-28)
75 Stony Creek Station (December 1)
76 Operations against Warren's Raid to Hicksford, Virginia (December 7-12)
77 Bellefield (December 9-10)
Appomattox Campaign (March 28-April 9, 1865)
78 Sutherland Station, Southside Railroad (April 2)
79 Scott's Cross Roads (April 2)
80 Prince Edward Court House (April 7)
81 Clover Hill/Appomattox Court House (April 9)
81 Surrender Appomattox Court House (April 9-12, 1865)

Chapter Four
Big Jane and Big Lucy

The first United States Census after the end of the War Between the States in 1870 reveals much about the Lesters of Henry County. William A. Lester, Sr. age 67 had real estate valued at $800 and personal property valued at $400. His wife, Frances age 61, lived with William A. and a wagoneer named Henry Pace and his wife. William Barrow was under the same roof with the Lesters. After the Civil War in 1870, an African-American Harriett Lester age 35, listed as a domestic servant was living in the home of William Lester. Living with Harriett Lester are Mary , a house servant, age 18, Woody, a male farm laborer, age 14, Latisha age 8, Jibby, a female age 5 and Eliza age 3. All listed as "B" for Black. The latter three listed as "at home."

Nearby was another head of household G. W. Lester, age 34, with real estate valued at $1,000 and personal property of $2,000. Living under his roof was Silas Bird, a 25-year-old laborer, B. Bowls, age 19, Booker Mitchell age 20 and John Williams age 21. All listed as laborers. The final person listed in the home of G. W. Lester was an African-American female age 30 listed as a "Cook."

The 1870 Census lists W. A. Lester, Jr. as a manufacturer. He married Susan Victoria Lovell (July 6, 1854-December 17, 1926) on January 11, 1872. This union produced five children including Ainsley Jackson, Mary Loula, Allye, Henry Clay Lester, and J. Randolph.

Other siblings of George Washington Lester I included Julia Ann Lester (1840-1897), who married William M. Barrow, the son of William and Susannah Marshall Barrow. The latter was the daughter of Samuel and Cassandra Alfriend Marshall. The connection to the Barrow Family paid dividends later to the Lesters especially to the son of G. W. Lester, George Tilden Lester. Another son was John Carlton Lester (1843-1898). Known for his civic responsibility Marshall Jackson Lester's (September 30, 1845-November 10, 1918) tombstone reads, "Upright and just he was in all his ways. A bright example in degenerate days." Sarah E. Lester (1853-1892) married H. G. Brown, a 24-year-old Salesman from Franklin County on June 10, 1872. Susan Virginia Lester (1854-1929) married Henry C. Pace, thirty-year-old "Teamster," the son of Daniel and Serena Pace, on January 10, 1870.

Also listed in the 1870 Census was Henry Clay Lester age 31, a tobacco manufacturer, with real estate valued at $3,000 and personal property valued at $10,000. Living with him were

William, a 35 year old "Clerk," a 19 year old named Sarah, Frank Griggs and twelve more African-Americans from age 11 to 24 listed as working in the tobacco factory.

Henry Clay Lester was born on February 25, 1838, in Henry County. He married Lucy Clark Brown, at age 16, on August 10, 1871. "Big Lucy" was born on May 6, 1855, to Frederick Rives and Elizabeth Cheedle Brown born on May 6, 1855.

Henry Clay Lester, the brother of George Washington Lester I, has his own remarkable story as businessman and leader in Henry County. This Lester comes down to us as a man of "frail physique," who hired an "Irishman" for $800 to serve as a substitute for him during the war. Lester said he was "not interested in fighting, but interested in enterprise." Asthma is a disease that is prevalent within the Lester Family continuing into the present generations. Known for his "dry humor," Henry like many of the Lester men had asthma. One writer described its use as a way to lighten "the burden of ill health."

Henry began a tobacco business after the War Between the States at Shady Grove and then at Figsboro. The community of Figsboro gets its name from plug tobacco brand name "Lester Fig." He did not trademark his product names so G. W. Lester used

"Lester Fig" as well. Henry had the "Midas Touch" with everything he touched turning to gold.

Today Shady Grove, Virginia, is a community that shows virtually no signs of the sprawling business area it was in the mid nineteenth century. A post office was in the community as early as January 20, 1820, with Benjamin Marshall acting as first postmaster. The post office continued there until February 13, 1904. The community located on the Danville Pike between Snow Creek and Martinsville was the site of tobacco manufacturing facilities including Henry Clay Lester, serving as Postmaster on October 21, 1868. The job at that time was a political appointment and the Republicans were still controlling the federal patronage.

There were fifteen tobacco manufacturing facilities listed in Franklin County in 1881-82 including five at Shady Grove operated by J. R. and F. R. Brown, J. P. Bondurant, F. Cook, George Washington Lester and Henry Clay Lester.

Henry Clay Lester diversified his business interests being a merchant, farmer with the Lanier Farms, Inc., handling livestock, and milling with the Lester Livestock and Grain Company, but most of all as a "tobacconist."

One story involves Henry C. Lester buying tobacco at one cent a pound when no one wanted it during one of the many economic downturns that were cyclical during the end of the nineteenth century. Lester filled every warehouse and space he could rent. English buyers later bought the tobacco for nine cents a pound making a 900% profit for young Lester. His tobacco brands included "Gold Fig, Little Alice, Belle of Henry, Black Joe, Trade Mark, Level Best and of course, Lester Fig."

A story from the livestock side of the business involved selling mules to local farmers on a monthly payment basis. Lester had a ride up window, the precursor to the drive up window of today, where the local farmers could come up to make their payments. When a farmer could not make a payment Lester allowed him more time to use the mule as he knew that if he took the animal the farmer had no way to generate the income needed to make the payment.

Charles P. Smith, Jr. worked for Henry Clay Lester and said he made 75 cents per day working sunup to sundown. "We had more money than we ever had since." Smith noted that Lester's teams never pulled an empty wagon. If it went one way with hay or wood, it returned with a load of manure or food.

After moving to Martinsville, H. C. Lester lived there for over twenty-six years, he constructed over 100 buildings along with three flourmills, and three saw mills in Henry County. He joined the Christian Church in Martinsville in 1884 and ten years later constructed a building at his own expense for the Broad Street

Christian Church. He built the Broadstreet Hotel that his wife converted to a hospital, the Lucy Lester Hospital, with her nephew in law Dr. Morton E. Hundley serving as chief surgeon. After Hundley's death, it reverted to being a hotel.

In 1885, Englishman George Pearson began to build Lester's home in downtown Martinsville. It contained twenty-two rooms. The home took three years to build and had fourteen-foot high ceilings with a fireplace in each room and a wrought iron entrance gate brought from England.

In 1914, Lester built a tapestry brick wall with granite caps and a wrought iron gate around the house. Two years later Lester returned from a trip to Florida to find a water pipe during a particularly cold snap broke and flooded the bottom floor, which Henry Clay Lester and Rives Brown Sr. turned into a "skating rink."

Henry Clay Lester's palatial home burned in 1946 and only the garage or stable as Lester knew it remains where the house that once took up the entire block bordered by Clay, Lester, and Main Streets in Martinsville. By the time of the fire, the home was a "Dormitory" that had thirty people living in it and operated by Drs. Doris Millikan. The fire department received a call at 2:50 a.m. James Murphy of Rocky Mount was working at Bassett Furniture and staying in the house. He saved a little boy, but apparently not his own shoes. Miss Irene Hall of Axton, was twenty-one and working at DuPont and only had time to grab her coat as she fled the burning house.

H. C. Lester not only had his own businesses, but was involved in many other regional enterprises serving as a President of Farmers Bank of Martinsville, Vice-President of the First National Bank of Martinsville when the former merged with the latter, Director of Virginia and North Carolina Construction and President and Director of the Danville and New River Railroad.

Although little information is available local historian Virginia Windle and others believed that Henry Clay Lester was involved in 1880 construction on another railroad coming from the east came through Henry County going west to what was then Taylorsville, now Stuart, Virginia. Starting on March 20, 1873, the Danville and New River Railroad began. By 1882, construction reached Martinsville and the following year Spencer had rail service. From August 1, 1884, until July 1942 rail service went from Danville to Stuart. One article states that when Henry County voted to "take stock in the railroad," Henry Clay Lester bought the county bonds giving the railroad bonds "high market value" and "assured the building of the railroad." Financial problems kept the railroad from stretching further across Patrick County. In 1886, bankruptcy caused the line to operate in receivership until 1891.

Purchase by bondholders, the railroad changed its name to the Danville and Western Railroad, the "Dick and Willie." The line became part of the Richmond and Danville Railroad and in 1894 part of the Southern Railway. The narrow gauge railroad became standard gauge in 1903. The last train on the line was an excursion running on October 1976.

Henry Clay Lester and the railroad that became the Winston-Salem/Roanoke Division of the Norfolk and Western Railroad, now Norfolk Southern Railroad, changed the face of Henry County and Martinsville. Another author wrote, "Without the railroad, the potential wealth of Henry County, its virgin forests, its winding streams, might have remained forever undeveloped and unproductive." The 122 miles of railroad track from Roanoke, Virginia, to Winston-Salem, North Carolina of "shining steel rails" known as the "Punkin Vine" because of the winding nature of the route reminded those involved of the curvy stalk of a pumpkin.

In February 1886, investors held an organization meeting of the Roanoke and Southern Railroad. The results of this meeting were two corporations formed in each state of Virginia and North Carolina. The Virginia group was led by President David F. Houston of the Crozer Iron Works, Henry Clay Lester as Vice-President, Secretary S. W. Jamison and Treasurer E. H. Stewart.

Officers of the North Carolina Corporation included R. J. Reynolds. The standard gauge railroad of 4 feet 8 inches stretches 122.53 miles consolidated on June 18, 1887 with a main office in Roanoke and an operational headquarters in Winston-Salem. Division B (Martinsville to Roanoke) started later than the North Carolina section. Grading began in Henry County in February 1888 from the north bank of Reed Creek to the Smith River. Trains began rolling in North Carolina on May 6, 1889, with the first train reaching Martinsville in April 1891. By January 1892 the line was open all the way.

One person who took advantage of the new railroad was a local grocer named John D. Bassett, who started a sawmill. He eventually built his own business that is today Bassett Furniture Corporation. Trains still roll through Bassett, Virginia, on the "Punkin Vine" carrying coal and other freight. Passengers rode the train until 1961.

Gunfire erupted in Tombstone, Arizona, on October 26, 1881, with the Earps and Doc Holiday taking on the Clantons and the Cowboys. Five years later on May 17, 1886, Martinsville, Virginia, saw one of the largest gunfights ever recorded on the east coast, a shootout that ended with nine shot and three dead including an African-American bystander.

Aiken Summit along the Danville and Western Railroad was home to the Terrys. Their home Mar's Hill and Terry's Mountain were marks they left on the landscape of Henry County, Virginia, but in the late 1880s traditions says their prospects were on the way down. The children of Parker and Mary King Terry lived on land literally granted them from colonial times. The Spencers were a family on the rise and in the summer of 1886. Their home was Grassdale these two families met as their lines of rise and dissent met on the streets of Martinsville.

D. H. Spencer and Sons moved their tobacco operation to Fayette Street within site of the Henry County Court House. Their brands included Calhoun and Old Crow. The company was one of the first to make their own boxes for shipment. Peter Spencer was on the Martinsville Town Council. On May 8, 1886, the council heard complaints from two fertilizers agents, A. W. Hill and B. F. Barrow, who thought their annual license tax discriminated against their product. They did not get the two-thirds vote needed to change their bill with Mayor C. B. Bryant and "Colonel Peter" Spencer voting against them.

The Editor of the Henry News, J. T. Darlington, published an anonymous article that was an obvious satire of the meeting. The article written by local attorney William King Terry, who may have represented the fertilizer agents, made fun of Bryant and

Spencer. On Saturday, May 15, Terry distributed a printed circular that was more critical of the two men. One author speculates that it looks like an "over reaction" or an "emotional" response by Terry that may indicate some existing bad blood between the Spencers and Terrys.

The following day, the story goes, May 16, a Sunday, Peter Spencer printed up his own poster comparing Terry to a jackass. John Hardin Pedigo, who apparently wrote for both sides, "ghost wrote" the poster. Attempts to destroy the posters were not completely successful as William Terry found one. "Finding himself effectively called an SOB, Will Terry was enraged." This was a time of honor and reputation in the two decades since the end of the Civil War and with the recent death of his father, Terry could not ignore the slander. He lived in a local hotel in Martinsville and the small world the town would have been at that time made conflict and stirring the pot of controversy was good sport for some in those days as cable television sensationalizes today's rumors and innuendo.

Where did he come from?
Nobody knows for sure,
But everybody know he's a jack of all trades
Where do jackasses come from?
Why, anybody knows a jackass come from

Another jack ass that's been rented all around the country."

Terry distributed another circular. The printer, probably Darlington at the Henry News, certainly was busy. It read, "I have been attacked by some low contemptable scoundrel and midnight assassin, by the publication of an anonymous card. If however he will present himself he shall receive the chasetisement he so richly merits."

On Monday, May 17, Terry learned that the Henry News printed Peter Spencer's circular. He sent word to his brothers and Jake and Ben Terry, who soon arrived on the railroad in Martinsville. Noting the heightened tension, more "peace officers" than usual were present including the Sheriff, several deputies, two constables, and a town sergeant.

At 7 p.m., employees streamed out of the Spencer Tobacco plant on Fayette Street, where they worked sunrise to sunset. When Peter and John Spencer came out, William Terry called and asked Peter directly if he wrote the "horse card." Peter answered that he did. Terry grabbed his pistol, but W. H. Werth grabbed Terry. John Spencer suggested that there were "other means for handling the dispute." J. T. Darlington pointed out that the Spencers outnumbered the Terrys, as the Spencers had five gunmen present due to "prior arrangements." Seeing the situation William Terry stepped way with Darlington.

As with all such situations it only takes one person to create a catastrophe and that person was Tarleton Brown. Smoke filled the air for about twenty-five feet around the entrance to the Spencer Tobacco Company. The Richmond Dispatch noted, "at least a dozen revolvers flashed in the air. The death dealing missiles flew thick and fast, rarely missing their prey. Every man stood his ground with nerve and grit." Gilmore Dickinson shot Will Terry in the back "fifteen inches away." Ben Terry shot Tarleton Brown after the latter fired at Jake Terry.

The shootout wounded nine people. All three Terry brothers were down. Jake died immediately, Will died after lingering several weeks and Ben, hit twice, once in the neck, recovered. Peter Spencer shot in the ribs survived for five years. Bystanders J. R. Gregory and an African-American Sandy Martin lost his life.

Shot were "Peace Officers" Hugh N. Dyer and B. L. Jones. Hugh Nelson Dyer went on to become Roanoke Chief of Police and wrote a memoir of the event. Born on November 28, 1860, in Henry County, the son of W. C. Dyer, Hugh served as a Police Chief and Sergeant for five years in Martinsville. He went to Roanoke in 1889 and on December 20, 1893, became the Chief of

Police. That same year he married Emma Hutchinson. He died on August 5, 1936, in Staunton and rests today in Roanoke's Fairview Cemetery.

The court fined Ben Terry $20 and costs for carrying a concealed weapon. A judge dismissed all other charges. The Terry daughters moved on top of Terry Mountain due to the shame of the shootout. None of the ten Terry children reportedly ever married.

Years later a magazine writer, Hiram Herbert, wrote a story for Saga Magazine: Adventure Stories For Men. When no locals would talk with him other than Gus Dyer, the son of Hugh, Herbert resorted to sensationalizing the story by interjecting a romance between May Belle Spencer or Belle Spencer and Will Terry.

Born in on September 16, 1861, Tarleton (Tarlton) F. Brown died on May 8, 1895, nearly a decade after the shootout on Fayette Street. After the death of Tarleton (Tarlton) Brown in 1895, and his wife Annie Eliza Brown (1862-1901) six years later, Henry Clay Lester and Lucy raised her brother's children Rives S. Brown, Lucy Brown "Little Lucy," and Mattie T. Brown. The latter married George M. Andes. When "Big Lucy" died she left the Lanier Farm to Rives and "Little Lucy."

Frederick Brown and his three brothers Reuben, John, and Tarleton came to Virginia in the mid 1700s. Tarleton married a "Miss Napier" and had a son named Tarleton, who married Lucy

Clark Moorman of Campbell County, Virginia. He too had a son named Tarleton, but Frederick is the progenitor of the line we are discussing. Frederick married a "Miss Stegall" and had a son named John, who married Sallie Rives, a great-granddaughter of Virginia Colonial Governor Alexander Spotswood. Their son, Frederick Rives Brown married Elizabeth Cheedle. They were the parents of Tarleton Brown, father of Rives Spotswood Brown.

Henry Clay Lester closed his tobacco factory in 1899. Today the site near Figsboro is behind Hundley's Southeastern Outdoor Supplies. Forty years later all signs of the Lester's time at Figsboro were gone except for the name of the community due to fire.

Henry Clay Lester lived until September 18, 1913. A Republican "by choice" he voted for the party of the President, Abraham Lincoln, his brothers fought against in war. The day of his funeral all the businesses in Martinsville closed as a sign of respect. A driver can see another sign of respect for the man who did so much for Martinsville on Highway 108 north of the entrance to Roselawn Cemetery on the left is Big Jane Street. "Big Jane" was the nickname of Henry Clay Lester although no one can tell this author why.

Rives Spotswood Brown, Sr. (1894-1957), a graduate of Randolph-Macon, became a prominent man of Martinsville. When

Henry Clay Lester died in 1913, Brown took over management of the Lester's business interest. On May 20, 1916, Brown married Cornelia Frances Gregory and they had a son Rives S. Brown, Jr. on August 30, 1919.

Rives S. Brown, Sr. began his first development on Mulberry Road in 1925. In 1930, Rives S. Brown, Sr. built the Chief Tassell Building and five years later the Rives Theatre, Kroger's Grocery, and the Greyhound Bus Station. Three years later in 1938, he came up with a plan for Forest Park.

Among other holdings inherited from Henry Clay Lester, "the wealthiest man in Henry County at the time," was the Lanier Farm that Brown farmed until 1922. The Marshall Hairston Lanier Farm had a storied history, which was once the property of Patrick Henry, who sold the property to David Lanier, until today where the 2,000 acres is the site of the Druid Hills and Forest Park residential areas. Brown moved to Mulberry in 1925 and enlisted the help of landscape architect Earle S. Draper. The development began in 1938 and two years later with arrival of DuPont development accelerated. During the 1930s-40s, architects Bryant Heard and William Roy Wallace built homes on the former Lanier Farm. In 1956, Lake Lanier developed and two years later Martinsville annexed the property. The former farm was a favorite place for horseback riding for many local children carrying the legacy of the Lester Family. In 1958, Druid Hills Shopping Centre came to life.

Lucy Gaines Brown "Little Lucy" (1888-1926) married Dr. Morton Elbridge Hundley. After Lucy's death, Dr. Hundley married Mary Kate Black (1896-1944) in November 1927 at the age of 49. Hundley died on his honeymoon of pneumonia in Switzerland. After his death Mary married John Phillips, the son of oil magnate Frank Phillips and lived in the Adolphus Hotel in Dallas, Texas.

The legacy of Henry Clay Lester lives on in the marks the two Rives Browns made on Henry County and the contributions their families continue to make on the landscape of Henry County Virginia.

Henry Clay Lester enjoying a ride around Martinsville

56

Henry Clay Lester and his home below.

Chapter Five
All Roads Lead To Waidsboro

Virginia created Franklin County in 1786. The man honored by this naming had sixty-three years earlier walked down Market Street in Philadelphia in 1723. Benjamin Franklin wrote of his walk down the street that began an 800-mile journey for many travelers all the way to the Savannah River between Georgia and South Carolina because Market Street was the beginning of the northern terminus for the Great Philadelphia Wagon Road.

"Then I walked up the street, gazing about till near the market-house I met a boy with bread. I had made many a meal on bread, and, inquiring where he got it, I went immediately to the baker's he directed me to, in Secondstreet, and ask'd for bisket, intending such as we had in Boston; but they, it seems, were not made in Philadelphia. Then I asked for a three-penny loaf, and was told they had none such. So not considering or knowing the difference of money, and the greater cheapness nor the names of his bread, I made him give me three-penny worth of any sort. He gave me, accordingly, three great puffy rolls. I was surpriz'd at the quantity, but took it, and, having no room in my pockets, walk'd off with a roll under each arm, and eating the other.

Thus I went up Market-street as far as Fourth-street, passing by the door of Mr. Read, my future wife's father; when she, standing at the door, saw me, and thought I made, as I certainly did, a most awkward, ridiculous appearance. Then I turned and went down Chestnut-street and part of Walnut-street, eating my roll all the way, and, corning round, found myself again at Market-street wharf, near the boat I came in, to which I went for a draught of the river water; and, being filled with one of my rolls, gave the other two to a woman and her child that came down the river in the boat with us, and were waiting to go farther.

Thus refreshed, I walked again up the street, which by this time had many clean-dressed people in it, who were all walking the same way. I joined them, and thereby was led into the great meetinghouse of the Quakers near the market. I sat down among them, and, after looking round awhile and hearing nothing said, being very drowsy thro' labor and want of rest the preceding night, I fell fast asleep, and continued so till the meeting broke up, when one was kind enough to rouse me. This was, therefore, the first house I was in, or slept in, in Philadelphia."

Called the Great Road or the Carolina Road, the road split off from what Daniel Boone called the Wilderness Road at present day Roanoke, Virginia, making a southern route for travelers such as the Moravians to reach Salem, North Carolina. Two hundred and eighty six years after Franklin made his walk, this author stood on the banks of the Savannah River in his mother's home town of Augusta, Georgia, some 750 miles from Franklin's Market Street in Philadelphia. The connection between these two sites is that they are on opposite ends of the "Great Philadelphia Wagon Road." Like many paths in the history of the Lester Family, all these roads lead to Waidsboro, Virginia, in Franklin County.

The "Road" was the ancient path for the Native Peoples including the Iroquois from New York, who used it to trade and attack the Carolina tribes such as the Tuscarora, Catawba, and Cherokee. Known by names such as the Appalachian Warrior Path, Great Indian Path, and the Shenandoah Hunting Path, the road became the route for Scots-Irish and Moravians on their way to present day Winston-Salem, North Carolina. The Treaty of Lancaster in 1744 between the English Colonists and Natives opened the route for the great migration that followed. The treaty "convinced the Six Nations to surrender their land to the "setting sun," which the Indian Confederacy interpreted as the crest of the Alleghenies and the British interpreted as all of western Virginia, to the Ohio River. With the road open travelers carried tobacco from the Carolinas to Baltimore, Maryland, and by 1763 it was open all the way to Georgia.

From Philadelphia, Pennsylvania, to Lancaster, York, and near a town named Gettysburg the road crossed into Maryland near Hagerstown and on into Virginia by Winchester. The road continued down the Shenandoah Valley by Staunton and Lexington to Big Lick, present day Roanoke, where the road turned south going into North Carolina near Bethenia, Salem, Salisbury, and Charlotte before entering South Carolina. From Rock Hill, Chester, and Newberry, South Carolina, the Great Philadelphia Wagon Road crossed the Savannah River into Augusta, Georgia.

Travel averaged ten miles a day. Modes of transportation included pack trains of up to twelve horses, stagecoaches with four to six horses. Animal trains of cattle, turkey, and sheep used the path. In 1753, the Moravians from Pennsylvania made their way in Conestoga Wagons, twenty-two feet long, five feet wide and twelve feet high, pulled by four to six horses or oxen. They described it as "no roads, only small paths, in many places grown up with grass and covered with leaves." In places they had to "hack out 12 miles just to continue."

Among those families that made their way along the road and stopped in Franklin County, Virginia, were the Waids. John Ferguson lived to their south and James Calloway to the north along "The Great Road." As generations passed one daughter

Victoria Frances Waid was born on November 3, 1856 to Creed and Elizabeth Turner Waid of Franklin County, just northwest of the Lester's home in Henry County. Victoria's brothers included William Powell Waid (1859-1939) and Thomas Archer Waid (1860-1939).

    Victoria's father Creed Watkins Waid (November 25, 1825-January 28, 1905) descended from Robert (1781-1834) and Anne Sandier Waid (ca.1788-ca.1850). Creed's siblings included Elizabeth, John, James, William, Naomi, Sophia, and Powell. Robert married Sue Walker Piccard after his first wife's death. They had three children including Duffy, John, and Clarence. Robert Waid operated the stagecoach inn and a tobacco plantation. He was the son of Moses Waid, born in 1751 in Henry County, and one of eight children. Moses married Fanny Ferguson, the daughter of John and Elizabeth Ferguson. The Fergusons owned the stagecoach inn before the Waids and sold it to Robert. Robert's father Moses was the son of Phillip Waid, who died in Prince Edward County, Virginia, in 1795. Phillip was the son of James Waid II and his wife Dorothy. James descended from another James Waid. New Kent County, Virginia, lists this original James Waid in 1704, where he had 150 acres.

    As early as December 26, 1795, travelers noted the presence of the Waid's along the "Old Carolina Road." Mr.

Johnston and friends "rode south of Fincastle, Botetourt County, Virginia, to Big Creek (Roanoke River)." "I got my horse shod from thence we rode 8 miles to a Widow Forgesons." They noted thirty Negroes at a "Ball" in the Negro house. Illegal in many places, the family was ahead of its time by teaching their slaves to read. "This was in Franklin County in the morning we cros'd Pigg River and Rode 4 miles. This was on Sunday the 28th of the…Breckfasted a Mr. Standford from there." Creed Waid married into the Standifer Family.

One visitor described the site of the Waid home as "Treasure Valley." "The King of the Golden River emerging from the dense forest through which an unimpaired road leads to the cultivated valley with the glittering river winding through, and the imposing white house in the center, the sight which greets the eye is one of surprising comfort and well being."

The home "well established at the old home place" sat two hundred feet from the Pigg River on a slight knoll that was a stagecoach stop along the "Great Wagon Road" was made of large hand dressed logs connected with wooden pegs. It was a T-shaped structure with two stories, a cellar, and a garret. Visible today are two chimneys built on the outside walls. There were two rooms on the first and second floors respectively with a fireplace in each room with a separate entrance to porch from each room. A central hall with a stairway contained closets underneath. A large parlor was to the right with a carved mantel and wide fireplace. A bedroom was on the left. The rear hall had two steps down that opened into a large dining room with a kitchen that had a long side porch. There was a long flag stone walk edged by box bushes.

The Waids attended Pleasant Hill Methodist Church. William A. Menefee married Naomi Jane Waid, who started the church. Even as an old man Creed W. Waid rode a horse eight miles to church.

It was Moses who "developed" the land along the Pigg River growing tobacco, grain, and apples along with horses and cattle. Franklin County lists Moses and his brother, Bartlett, in 1786 on the original tax rolls. Moses owned land from the Pigg River to Briar Mountain near Sydnorsville. Moses also had business in Rockingham County, North Carolina. Robert received the house after Moses. In 1852, Creed W. Waid got the house from Robert's heirs. In 1900, Creed deeded the house to his daughter Ella W. Hooker.

One writer of Franklin County history wrote of the early settlers. "They became mighty hunters, skilled in the use of firearms and traps of various kinds. The court records of the county tell of bounties paid them for wolves heads, hawks and other marauders…the Waid brothers were famed as marksmen."

Life at the Waid Stagecoach Inn included other residents. Among them was a goat that liked to sleep in a feather bed. A war of wills erupted between Creed Waid and the animal. The former used a broom as a weapon when he found the animal asleep in a feather bed. Unknown to the animal's nocturnal habits, two grandsons, Norman age 13 and Charlie age 10, arrived late at night with their father from Roanoke and went to bed. The two woke suddenly with the sound of "squeeeeeeak" as their bedroom door opened. They were even more surprised when the animal jumped into bed practically mugging the terrified Norman, who was shaking under the covers of his bed.

With the end of the Civil War and the lack of travel along the "Great Road," Creed W. Waid faced financial problems. He sold off land each year to pay property taxes. He became very much aware of saving every dime. One story says he stored food in a "larder" off the kitchen and it remained locked except for each morning when Waid took the key he carried and gave food to the cook for the day's meals. Many of the Waids left the area going as far away as Missouri, Oklahoma, and Texas.

At the end of the War Between the States, George Washington Lester I was thirty-one years old traveling home in June to Henry County, Virginia, from the prison at Point Lookout, Maryland. The 1870 Census had the bachelor living along the

Lester Branch of Beaver Creek as a "farmer" and "tobacconist." That changed three years later when he married Victoria Frances Waid on November 17, 1873, at Dyer's Store. She sold her share in the Waid Stagecoach Inn for $150.00 to her father's half brother Clarence who continued at the ancestral home. Today, the site is the Waid Recreational Area that includes soccer and baseball fields along with historical interpretation that denotes the "Great Road" that brought people to the banks of the Pigg River. The remains of two chimneys and a few outbuildings are the only remains of the Waid's time there.

The union of George Washington Lester I and Victoria Waid produced eight children. Walter Waid Lester was born on March 10, 1873. George Tilden Lester was born on September 14, 1876. Thomas Oscar Lester was born on March 7, 1878. Elizabeth Pearl Lester was born on January 14, 1880. Frances Susan Lester was born on October 31, 1881. Powell Jackson Lester was born on November 8, 1883. Loury Lawson Lester was born on February 6, 1886. Sarah Victoria Lester was born on February 21, 1896.

Walter Waid Lester (March 10, 1875-December 21, 1904) married Mary Lucy Davis, the daughter of E. W. and Elyn Davis (February 2, 1878-March 3, 1930) on February 8, 1893. This union produced five children: Sarah Victoria born in 1894, Lucy Waid born in 1896, and Ethel Claire born in 1898. (This lady supplied

Franklin County Historian Linda Stanley a wedding dress. This story is in the Acknowledgements.) Frances Golden was born in 1900 and followed by Jackson Pierpont in 1903. Family tradition states that Walter Waid Lester was an alcoholic and that disease caused his early death.

    G. W. and Victoria Waid Lester's daughter Elizabeth Pearl Lester born on January 14, 1880, married three times. The third marriage to G. T. Richardson on January 31, 1900, produced seven children: John Armstrong, Reeves, Elizabeth, Daisie, Jesse, Charles, and Victoria Richardson.

    Frances Susan Lester born on October 31, 1881, married Andrew Wade Patterson (March 29, 1875-December 16, 1958) on January 21, 1904, and produced seven children: Frances Victoria, Loula Pearl, Lucy Elizabeth, Lewis Andrew, George Richardson, Helen Angel, and Zella Mary. Frances died on January 24, 1950.

    Thomas Oscar Lester was born March 7, 1878. He married Margaret F. Craig, age 17, of Franklin County on January 24, 1900. Described as very beautiful and artistic, the lady who made "beautiful clothes," Margaret had five children George S., Gladys, Frank Victor, Dorothy, and Burton. A niece described "Uncle Oscar" as a "sweet person as long as he stayed away from the creature." A weakness for alcohol was a trait shared by men of the

Lester men that destroyed many, but many learned from the example.

Powell Jackson "Uncle Jack" Lester born on November 18, 1883, and married Maize Martin, a descendent of Joseph Martin. Described as "one of the most Christian ladies I have ever met," Maize and Jackson shared a love "most people never do." Their children were Martin Jackson, George Milton, Thomas Lawson, John Reid, Eliza Victoria, Powell Ray, and Thomas Burton Lester. Known for never swearing, Jack said "By-Guineas!" He later moved to Spencer where he died on February 25, 1944.

Loury Lawson Lester, born on February 6, 1886, married Mamie F. Draper (July 29, 1889-January 26, 1935) on September 21, 1909. They had eight children: Lowry Lawson, Victor Arlington, Ralph Clayton (the subject on another chapter in this book), Golden Mary, Mamie Vauline, Inez Mattie, Lottie Lee, and Virginia Joy.

A son, Reeves William Lester (1889-1893), came next. Sarah Victoria Lester born on February 21, 1896, married Vaughn Minter Draper on September 12, 1914. They had three children: Lester Vaughn, June Victoria, and Mack Randolph Draper. Sarah died in 1981 with eight grandchildren and twelve great-grandchildren.

After the war George Washington Lester farmed growing tobacco and continuing his life as a "tobacconist." He told his children "Nobody would lend me any money to get started, so I made my own way by working." He farmed, worked with his brother Henry Clay Lester, and then started his own tobacco factory, apple brandy distillery, and gristmill.

In 1872, he bought 214 acres on Leatherwood Creek at Dyer's Store from C. Y. Thomas including a "brick factory" built by Captain Zephniah "Zef" Stultz. Lester manufactured plug chewing tobacco shipping his product as far away as Baltimore and Philadelphia. He diversified his business interests developing water powered flour and saw mills. Before 1898, when it closed, his distillery produced the Lester Brand of Apple Brandy. Before prohibition in the twentieth century producing spirits was a business that many people legally participated in. It is a time nearly forgotten when chestnuts still dominated the hardwood forests and their nuts were so plentiful that they were a commodity used to feed livestock or barter for merchandise.

A granddaughter of George Washington and Victoria Waid Lester described their home at Dyer's Store "quite showy." The Lesters were toiling upward in the years after the war. They cut flowers on Fridays for the weekends. Their home had an organ, beautiful chairs, and a table with a bric-a-brac that held the family bible. There was a big swing on the porch where a granddaughter remembered watching the humming birds. The house had four large rooms, two upstairs and two downstairs with a long dining room, a kitchen with two storage rooms behind it.

The tobacco factory was three stories made of handmade brick. Many family members reported "Ghosts" in the building. Vickie Waid Lester and a granddaughter once heard someone walking on the floor above them, but no one was there. An image on a windowpane supposedly resembled Captain Stultz, who built the factory. There were many buildings in the complex including a stable for the horses, a barn for animals and their feed. No one killed black snakes as they ate the rats that ate the animal food. There was a well in a shed, a buggy house, an icehouse and a mill grinding wheat and corn.

Described as "not mechanical," G. W. Lester nearly lost it all. The root of his problems was a kind heart and not tough enough business acumen. He co-signed financial notes for friends and family and when those people shrunk from their responsibility, George W. Lester owed the money. He told his children "Don't ever go on anybody's note. You see what it has done to our family." It forced G. W. to sell off his assets leaving at his death only the tobacco operation. No doubt the stress of the situation contributed to his poor health and asthma condition led to invalidism and his death of pneumonia on January 20, 1898, just before his sixty-second birthday. Victoria Waid Lester found herself widowed at age 42 with eight children, but she had strong children, who cared for her and continued to make their mark on Henry County, Virginia.

The Waid House in Franklin County, Virginia

71

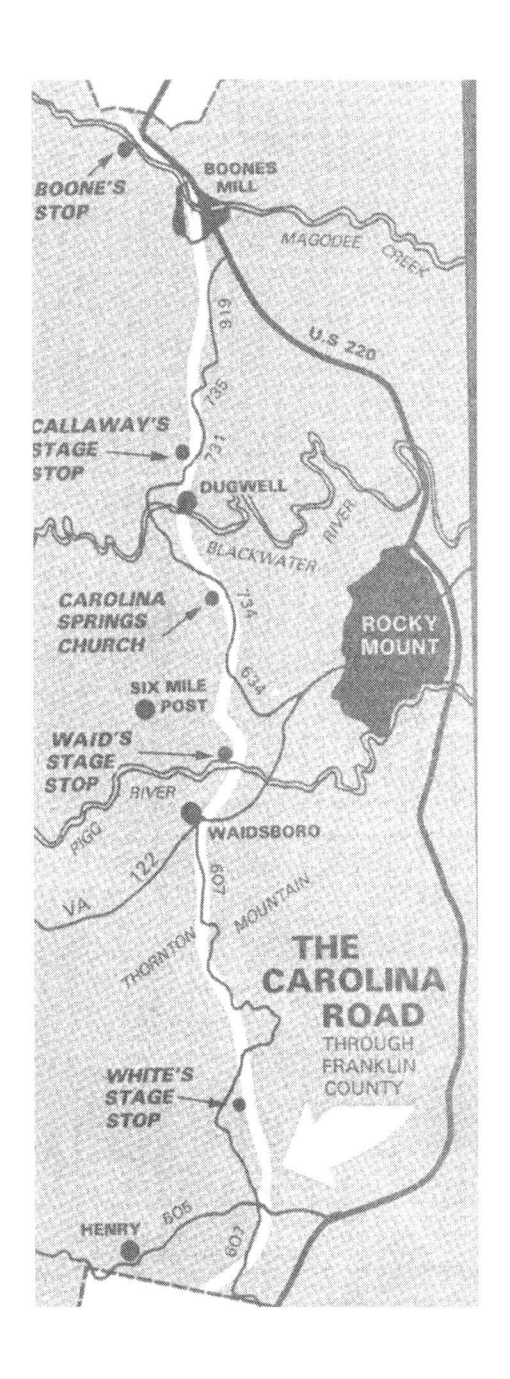

The Carolina Road remnants and the graves of the Waids at the park that bears their names in Franklin County, Virginia.

Chapter Six
Tobacco, Timber and Parker

Born the second child of George Washington and Victoria Ann Waid Lester in 1876 at Dyer's Store in northern Henry County, George Tilden Lester became a bigger than life figure known to all as "Cap'n Til."

George Tilden Lester grew up in the rural isolation of Dyer's Store. He walked to a one-room school two to three miles every day. Young George dropped out of school in the fourth grade. At the age of ten, he became his father's bookkeeper and he kept an eye on the family business for the next eighty years. Even late in life he had the mail for his company brought to him believing that no one could ever cheat him as long as he knew when and where the money was coming from.

He began his business life after his father's death $4,000 in debt. "My father was an honest man and debts bothered him. He made me promise to raise the family and pay off the debts."

His tobacco chewing tobacco or plug business had brands such as GTL, GTL Three Ply, and Hotcake. "Cap'n Til" was thought to be the first man to "prime tobacco," which was the process of harvesting the plant by moving up the plant over the summer as the leafs became ripe rather than taking the entire plant at once.

In one of the few surviving letters from the family, Victoria Waid Lester wrote her brother Powell on August 24, 1905. "The boys will soon be young men. I hope they will be good boys and help you. Do not work all the time. I think you could spare a few days to come to see me. I am sorry to hear your health is bad. We are all tolerably well. Tilden and Jack are busy working tobacco. They have a nice lot of it. Oscar and Lowry are farming. Pearl and Fannie are very well. They have a fine boy apiece."

George Tilden Lester invented and patented a plug tobacco machine that sped up the production of the product. This was only one of two inventions out of many that he chose to patent. He used the proceeds from the sale of the patent that made 24 plugs at a time for $10,000 to get out of the debts ($4,000) he inherited from his father. The Lester-Adams Machinery Company of Baltimore, Maryland, owned by G. T. Lester and W. Brocke Tunstall, created to manufacture and marketed the "Plug" machines. (The patent application is at the end of this book.)

William Brocke Tunstall (1856-1917) was the son of Norfolk physician, Robert Baylor Tunstall (1818-1883) and Elizabeth W. Williamson (1821-1872). W. B. Tunstall's biography states that he was in the tobacco business in Baltimore. He married Eleanor Pratt Turner (1861-1937).

Lester spent time in the Washington/Baltimore areas to sell and install machinery. Eventually, as stated, he sold his interest in the company to come back to Henry County to devote his energies full time to the lumber business he started. The patent application is at the end of this book.

In 1905, Albert Einstein had his miracle year, where he imagined riding a beam of light to get his famous "Theory of Relativity." While George Tilden Lester was not a physicist, he like Einstein was able to visualize his world in a way to create inventions and solve problems relating to his business operations. Lester may have suffered from dyslexia, but he forced himself to focus on these designs and like Einstein he made a mark on his world.

Described as "a genius for mechanical invention and the operation of machinery" gave George Tilden Lester his start in life," George Tilden Lester was different from his father George Washington Lester I. Young Lester had "natural ability" with machinery. He had the gift to see things three dimensionally, a trait that proved very useful throughout his professional life. He could adapt machinery whether on the farm or in the lumber operation to diversified jobs. For example his father purchased a "left handed" sawmill. Young George took the challenge of converting the sawmill to right handed operation.

On March 6, 1896, George Tilden Lester became the sole proprietor of the Lester Lumber Company beginning a business that exists to this day. His operation began near Barrow's Mill using waterpower for a small saw and planning mills. Sawing at Barrow's Mill used the water of Beaver Creek using a metal pipe that was still in place until 1944. A flood destroyed the dam after a storm after the turn of the twentieth century. Mill parts remained until the 1930s and the pipes finally left the site over a hundred years after operations began there. Ralph C. Lester remembers attending a baptism in 1925 at the millpond of several acres. Recreation was another benefit of the mill. Ralph's father Loury swam "buck naked" in the water and had "great sport" catching turtles and eels.

On May 11, 1829, Henry County granted permission to William Barrow to build a water gristmill on the "South Fork of Leatherwood Creek." Barrow built on Beaver Creek instead beginning operation in 1830-31. Over the next hundred plus years owners beginning with Benjamin Barrow (1843-70), Peter T. Barrow (1870-77), Jesse Turner (1877-1903), and William L. Barrow (1903-15) operated a mill on the site. Today, Lester Lumber Company owns the site of the mill that gave birth to the company. Described as an "active and large operation," from 1836 until 1892, the mill had "hundreds of customers grinding and sawing" buying merchandise, meal, flour and brandy at 75 cents a gallon came through the door.

It began with William Brown's plantation Flint Hill along Beaver and Leatherwood Creeks. Deeded to Samuel Marshall on May 1, 1799, it became the property of his son-in-law William Barrow, the husband of Susannah Marshall. William Marshall Barrow (1815-1877) married the sister of George Washington Lester I, Julia Ann Lester. They later moved to Washington County, Virginia, in 1860 and Rome, Georgia, in 1875. This connection to Barrow's Mill became very useful for the son of G. W. Lester, George Tilden "Cap'n Til" Lester.

George Tilden Lester married France Parker Turner on April 20, 1904. Their honeymoon trip to Niagara Falls delayed 2 ½ years included a business trip to deliver to Canada in person his plug tobacco machine. Described as "strong and brawny as a farm boy," George T. Lester was amused when customs officials asked him to lift the machinery for inspection.

Frances Parker Turner Lester was the daughter of Private C. M. Turner of Company F, 42nd Virginia Infantry. He was the son of Andrew and Frances Holland Turner. Turner found himself embroiled in battle in Orange County, Virginia on November 27,

1863, known as Mine Run. Suddenly a piercing pain hit his arm. It was his fourth wound of the two-year war, but this one took his arm. He was a member of Thomas J. "Stonewall" Jackson's Second Corps in the Army of Northern Virginia fighting the high tide of the Confederacy at Chancellorsville and after Jackson's death under Richard S. Ewell at Gettysburg.

Callohill Minnis Turner married Julia Anne Menefee of Franklin County in 1865. Five years later Turner was in Big Lick, now Roanoke, manufacturing plug tobacco with Henry and John Trout at Turner, Trout and Company. For twelve years he toiled upward building a life for his family of eight children.

Callohill Turner, the youngest son of Andrew (1797-1882) and Frances Holland Turner (1801-1900), was born on July 13, 1839. Frances was the daughter of Major John M. Holland, who represented Franklin County in the Virginia Legislature. Their children included William born in 1825, May born in 1827, John born in 1829, James born in 1831, George born in 1833, Andrew born in 1835, and Sarah born in 1837.

C. M. Turner served two terms on the Big Lick Town Council before receiving appointment to Town Assessor. When Roanoke incorporated in 1884, the people elected Turner the first Commissioner of the Revenue, where he served for ten years until retirement. He had houses on Henry Street, Franklin Road and eventually a twenty-acre farm south of the Roanoke River. He was a member of the Oscola Lodge of the Knights of the Pythians and a member of the Primitive Baptist Church. Every night he pulled up the cannonballs of his 1788 clock to rewind it.

Julia Anne Menefee described as a "Godly Methodist Lady," who became so full of the Holy Spirit that she shouted at church meetings. Their house in Roanoke had a huge entrance hall with a living room on the right and a library on the left. She had a photo viewer that allowed you to look through two lenses to visit far off people and places.

Julia Menefee was the daughter of William and Naomi Jane Waid Menefee. She was the granddaughter of Robert and Anne Standifer Waid, who ran the Waid Stagecoach Inn in Franklin County discussed in another chapter of this book. Julia Menefee Turner was of the "Pleasant Hill" Menefees. She had two brothers killed in the Civil War, William and Henry. A sister, Bettie, married Abram Holland, and a brother Creed Lee Menefee.

William Addison Menefee, Jr. enlisted on March 15, 1862, to Company D, 2nd Virginia Cavalry Regiment, the Franklin Rangers. Standing six foot tall with brown eyes and brown hair, he lost his life at Trevillian's Station on June 25, 1864, fighting under Wade Hampton, who replaced J. E. B. Stuart as leader of Robert E. Lee's cavalry. William took a slave to war as a "valet." Joe

Menefee stayed with the army and "proudly told everyone he was a Confederate Veteran."

The Menefees came to Franklin County with an uncle, William Crump. Crump built Pleasant Hill in 1804 and lived there until 1845 with his nephew George Menefee and his wife, the former Mary Rigney. George's father was William Menefee, who married Virginia Crump. William was the son of a Reverend Menefee and the grandson of Lt. Jonathan "Jonas" Menefee, who came to America during the American Revolution with his brother John as a member of the British Army. He switched sides and took an oath of allegiance on October 3, 1777, to the patriot cause. Among the nine children born to George and Mary was William A. Menfee, who married Naomi Jane Waid.

The Waid and Lester families continued to intermarry then and into present generations. George Tilden Lester, Jr. married Annie Sue Waid, the daughter of Clarence and Mary Angle Waid. Clarence was a half brother to Victoria Waid Lester, the children of Creed W. Waid with different mothers.

Turner and Julia had children beginning with Della, who married Frank Wickline and lived in Washington D. C. Morton W. Turner was the next child of Callohill and Julia Menefee Turner.

C. M. Turner remembered his great-grandfather, who was born in 1753. Turner possessed the first dollar he earned. It was a

Mexican dollar he got at age 12 for going to a local mill. Turner gave it to G. T. Lester, Jr., but he let Uncle Morton Turner borrow it and never got it back.

Morton Turner was a banker who lived on Highland Avenue in Roanoke. "When he got excited his wits became dull." Born in 1869, Morton attended Roanoke and Alleghany Institute before spending twelve years as an assistant to his father working as a treasurer and tax collector. He then spent two years at the Century Bank followed by sojourn at the Norfolk and Western Railroad before having eleven years in real estate with Turner and Turner. He was then President of Roanoke Banking Company, Vice-President of Roanoke Enameling and Stamping and the same position at Fidelity Realty.

Other children of C. M. Turner included Henry Turner, who moved to Johnson City, Tennessee, and had two daughters Elton and Ruth. Roy C. and William A. Turner died in infancy. The last girl born to Callohill and Julia was Frances Parker Turner on May1, 1880. Frances lost her mother Julia Menefee Turner when she was young.

C. M. Turner remarried to Lydia Emily Lowe on April 3, 1901, after Julia's death. She was a strict Presbyterian, who believed that you did not work on Sundays. She made all her food for the Sabbath Day on Saturday. There was no hot breakfast on Sunday and she made biscuits on "what looked like a stump."

The first child of George Tilden and Frances Parker Turner Lester, Julia Ann Lester, was born to George Tilden and Frances Parker Turner Lester on April 20, 1906. Julia Lester will give this narrative much of the color and flavor that just talking about men and business sorely lacks. Whoever sat her down for interviews published and otherwise has the eternal gratitude of this author.

Parker was not fond of her stepmother and before her own marriage she often visited her sister Della in Washington, D. C. Instead of meeting Parker in Henry County or Roanoke, it may be that George Tilden Lester encountered Parker while in the Washington/Baltimore area manufacturing and marketing his plug tobacco machine for the Lester and Adams Company.

If her photos are any indication Frances Parker Frances Turner was a beautiful woman. The daughter of Callohill M. Turner and his wife the former Julia Menefee received an inheritance from her father, but her brothers (William, John, James, George, and Andrew) did not. Turner supposedly believed that since he had made his way in the world with one arm that his sons could do much better with two, but his daughters needed him to help them and he did. Either way the Lester Family tradition is that she came to the marriage with George Tilden "Cap'n Til"

Lester possessing many qualities including a substantial inheritance from her father that helped the fledgling Lester Lumber Company prosper.

A visit to the Turners in Roanoke for the Lester children from Henry County was an adventure. The house had porches all around the house. Julia remembered, "At night I would go upstairs and look out the bedroom window to watch the big train with big lights coming down the track." A visit to the "Grandfather Callie" meant treats like raspberry ice cream and pound cake, rides on streetcars, and a chauffeur named James hauling you around. The Turners had electricity. Saturday nights often included a trip up Mill Mountain to watch the dances. Julia said the "lights were gorgeous to a country girl." Ladies danced in long dresses with large feathered fans, sitting at tables eating ice cream in little silver dishes. The scene was "too beautiful for words." "This was a thing of splendor for a little girl from the saw mill country." Visits to Roanoke included a trunk full of clothes, as you had to change twice a day while there. She remembered rides in a two-seated buggy with a colored man in uniform driving the vehicle. He tied the horse to a lion's head with a ring in its mouth.

Like her mother Frances Parker, Julia Lester visited Washington to see Aunt Della. They lived on B Street and could see the U. S. Capital Building. Julia remembered heavy barred entrance doors and beds that "folded and bolted down for sleeping." Julia loved to "sit on the steps and look at the Capitol" and she remembered eating her first shredded wheat biscuit and bananas. The furniture had inlaid marble and was upholstered. There were gaslights and Della held séances. The attic was a fascinating place and as the bedrooms were on the upper floors, Julia Lester would sneak up to the top of the house. There were sleeping porches and no refrigeration, so spoilable items stayed outside in "protected areas."

Morton Turner helped Julia Lester get over stage fright once. When Parker's daughter found herself on stage without knowing her part, she ran off crying. Uncle Morton Turner "schooled her in public speaking." Julia remembered Sundays at Morton. You went to church or you had a house call from the doctor. There were big dinners served, but nothing served stronger than tea or coffee. After lunch the children could read for a half hour in the library.

Parker had a son who died at birth. "Cap'n Til" buried his son at the Lester Family Cemetery at Dyer's Store with his father and mother. In 1928, Ralph Lester remembers being present at age 8 as a block wall went around the cemetery so that animals could not disturb the burying ground.

George Tilden Lester in 1903 began a portable logging and sawmilling operation powered by steam at Dyer's Store. At this time, he closed the tobacco company inherited from his father and concentrated his efforts on the lumber business.

In 1906, Julia Lester Oakley reported that the family moved to Gravely Street in Martinsville, but returned to Dyer's Store to live with Grandmother Victoria Waid Lester. Victoria suffered a double tragedy within a month at the end of 1904. On December 2, her son Walter Waid Lester passed away. On January 1, 1905, Victoria's father Creed W. Waid died. She started to Waidsboro for the funeral, but upon arrival at Sydnorsville, her brother John Lewis Waid's home, she learned the family already buried her father.

In 1908, George left the Dyer's Store area turning full time to lumber. Family tradition holds that he turned down as much as $5,000 annually by another tobacco company to devote himself full time to the lumber operation. Among the suitors interested in Lester's tobacco acumen was R. J. Reynolds. Lester said later in life, "I told him (Reynolds) I could make a living with tobacco and for that reason didn't want to sell the Fig Brand…I was a fool not to sell."

G. T. LESTER, SR.

George Tilden "Capt'n Til" Lester above and below George Washington Lester Tobacco Factory near Dyer's Store in Henry County, Virginia.

Chapter Seven
Finney Woods to Jones Creek

Portable logging began for George Tilden Lester in a stand of "virgin timber" in Franklin County called the "Finney Woods" or "Flat Woods." He paid the Finneys 400 silver dollars to mine the "original timber." This area had an "easy grade" and was so old that little undergrowth cluttered the area. In fact, "a buggy could be drive through the forest."

George T. Lester moved "everything and everyone to the Finney Woods." A community developed around the logging operation near Snow Creek in Franklin County that included lodging and meals for the crew. Employees lived in shacks and bunkhouses without houses, barns, stables, blacksmith shop and a commissary.

Parker adapted to life in the "Finney Woods." George and Parker lived in a house using slabs for weatherboarding that made little impression from the outside, but the inside was a different story. While the home of George and Parker was "very rustic" on the outside, the inside was spic and span. Jackson Lester said, "Outside it looks like a cow house, but on the inside it looks like a Vanderbilt House." With white ruffled curtains, wallpaper covered in violets with green and tan Chinese matting on the floors.

Parker's mother Julia Menefee Turner was of French descent and was "an artist with a needle" working with flowery needlework.

The family of George and Parker began to grow with George Tilden Lester, Jr. coming into the world in 1910 at the "Finney Woods" on May 20. His sister Julia said that her brother was afraid of her doll that had long eyelashes that G. T. Lester, Jr. thought it looked like fuzzy worms. Another neighbor boy was fascinated by Julia's "Teddy Bear" that growled. He cut the stuffed animal open to see how it worked. It was just a few years after Teddy Roosevelt left the White House. The President on a hunting trip to Mississippi refused to shoot a motherless bear cub and gave birth to the bear that still bears his name.

Julia remembered the wagon rides to Martinsville on Fridays with her mother, Parker, to pick up the payroll for the employees. The trip to the First National Bank in Martinsville to pick up the silver "Cap'n Til" paid his employees with was thirty-two miles round trip from the Snow Creek site of the lumber company. Julia remembered the money sitting between them and the revolver too. Parker was an "excellent markswoman," who practiced. They used hot rocks and wool blankets to keep them warm during the trip.

The size of the trees in the "Finney Woods" called for some innovations such as welding two cross cut saws together into one saw so that two men could cut down the hardwoods mainly of oak. The portable sawmill used a band saw and George T. along with Maston Martin did the sawing. Working dawn to dusk six days a week, oxen, mules and horses moved the timber on wagons "lumber trucks." The sawed lumber sat on strips and air-dried. Plow handles, plow beams, siding and rafters were the products gleaned from the "Finney Woods." In the early years of the twentieth century, the mill went to the timber and not the other way as it is today with timber coming to the mill.

In 1912, Lester Lumber Company "Til and his gypsies" moved to Figsboro into the "Happy Hollow." The area along what Ralph C. Lester calls the Lester Branch of Beaver Creek was the original home of the Lesters in Henry County. Nearby hundreds of acres and millions of feet of lumber came out of the "Hairston Woods," over the next twelve years. Today, this is the site of Patriot Centre Industrial Park and Patrick Henry Community College.

G. T. Lester, Sr. "Cap'n Til" bought his first car and a "Kelly" truck to haul timber. The car ran fine as long as it did not rain. If the "carbides" got wet, the lights went out on the vehicle. The roads were poor and Newton's law of motion became the norm that once you got the lumber truck in motion, keep it in motion and hope that the external force of mud did not stop the truck.

Another self-sufficient community developed at Figsboro around the lumber operation with a sawmill powered by wood fired boiler that made plow handles. There was a gristmill, maintenance shop, office with a storefront or commissary that sold produce making it more convenient for employees than traveling into town and a lumber plant. Across the creek, the Lester Branch of the Beaver Creek, Lester built a building to store wagons and later trucks. Returning near the old Lester home site gave some the opportunity to use older homes. G. T. Lester built homes for special employees or "Key People" such as Jackson Donalty and "Cab" Rumley, Will Flood "Buck" Belton, Cleve Coleman, Daniel Hundley, and a house on top of the hill for "Possum" Holland, who lived with his mother. The latter a "Colored Girl" helped Parker with her house especially in the kitchen.

George Tilden Lester built Parker an "adequate house" later occupied by Loury Lester until 1925 and was where Ralph Clayton Lester was born. Later this house became the home of "Sill," the cook, who was "piece by piece turned it into a barn." This home had a front and back room with a large hall, two bedrooms, dining room, kitchen, pantry and a maid's room. There were wood heaters and a big cook stove. This last house on the road like all the others had a water spring.

Parker was a "very efficient person" who nursed the sick, embalmed the dead, and visited the neighbors. She got screens on the windows to improve the health of the families and boiled water when lots of rain fell to protect everyone from germs. She was very careful to keep bed bugs out of the houses. Often after nursing the sick, Parker undressed on the back porch and had her own clothes boiled in a tub of carbolic acid so as not to bring disease into her house.

Every afternoon in good weather, a worker brought up a horse and buggy and tied it up to the house. Julia Lester reported that she and her mother "went a lot" on rides. If the roads were dusty, they wore long coats with veils over their hats. If someone needed a doctor, someone placed a saddle on Parker's horse because the animal's training told it to head to Martinsville. Mr. Donnely and Cab Rumley would go for the doctor when needed.

Parker made Julia's dresses with handmade flowers on them. Aunt Della in Washington sent hair ribbons and sashes. Even Parker's maid dressed in clothes from Washington, D. C. Julia remembered watching her dress on Sundays. She looked like the "Queen of Sheba." Aunt Della was very dark and beautiful, who walked straight in dresses with little trains made of beautiful colors and strings of bright beads.

"Cap'n Til" built bridges across the creeks. Parker could identify the approaching rider by the sound of hooves on the bridges. Parker had "ancorias" chickens, which were game animals and lacked the sense to roost in the trees. Parker often borrowed a neighbor's, Mrs. Horsley, blue hen. She traded eggs and bought produce from Horsley. Black and white, they never went to the chicken house. On cold nights, Parker mixed red pepper with their food to keep them warm.

Parker had a flower pit with shelves and a ladder with planks over it. She did the florist work herself. Julia Lester said that "Possum" would put flowers in the pit and when the sun came up he removed the planks to expose the plants to the sun and replaced it in the evenings. Then a rabbit cage sat on top of the planks. There were two rabbits a black and a white one. They trained their dogs not to run the rabbits. A dog named Doctor lived with the Lesters. "Cap'n Til" was not fond of dogs and Doctor was not fond of African-Americans, so it was quite a surprise for Lester when the dog went missing and he found him at a nearby "Black Man's."

Parker, like her daughter Julia, was a fan of bananas. She had fans for church with bananas on them. Once a "Black Girl" came to the house saying it was "hot as Hades in the church with a tin roof" and that she wanted a "flip flop," a fan, to fight off the heat.

"Cap'n Til" and Parker had a partnership in life and business. She kept the books until her third child, May, was born. After that Nick Prillaman took over as he also ran the commissary at Figsboro. The people respected the very organized Parker Turner Lester. Her daughter said, "Everyone loved her."

Julia Lester fondly remembered the days at Figsboro although not without a few painful lessons learned. Mr. Charlie Hundley had a peach and cherry orchard. He told Julia she could have fruit anytime she wanted. She came home one day with a peach and her father told her to take it back as it was stealing. She feared attack by wildcats and the screeching of owls did not help her cause as the sun went down to return the fruit. Julia told that her cousins Gladys and Fannie, children of "Cap'n Til's" sisters "caused me to get quite a few iris prints on my backside."

Christmas was a special time for the Lesters at Figsboro. Parker had a tree set up in the guest room with handmade ornaments, strings of popcorn and cranberries. "Cap'n Til" saved aluminum foil to make a star for the top of the tree. There were ginger bread angels and candles. The children got oranges, stick candy, sugarplums, and bon bons. Roman candles shot up into the air. A worker struck the dried out bladder of a hog with an ax to make a loud noise that was the signal to come for Christmas.

During the summer they held ice cream and cake suppers. "Possum," who was an African-American, hung Japanese lanterns in the pines and made seats using nail kegs with planks connecting them for people to sit on during these times. Lester held picnics for the employees and their families. "Cap'n Til" put straw on the "Wonder Kelly Truck" for rides to and from the picnics. Parker made sure that the "Colored Children" were included. Parker loved to take walks in the woods and her daughter said that she gave them a "rich heritage." "She never tired of doing good deeds for people."

The water springs had boxes built so that the cold water could pass through them to keep the food fresh. On Saturday nights, you took a bath in a cedar tub with water caught in a rain barrel or carried from the spring. During the summer, everyone washed clothes at the spring.

The entire village went to all day church services on Sunday and lived "like one big family." Baptisms caused workers to dam up creeks. Parishioners brought a large tub of sugar and lemons to church. Upon arrival, they unwrapped a wool cover revealing a block of ice and placed it in the tub.

It was a six-day workweek for the Lester Lumber Company with Sunday off for the employees. In 1924, Ralph Lester remembered carrying his father, Loury, lunch. He carried a large thermos of coffee and a gallon bucket of food. Ralph noted that his mother was "the best cook!" It was 1 ½ mile from the house to the portable mill. Ralph remembers his "Hot, Dirty and Kindly" talks with his father, who was the "Woods Superintendent," who worked ten-hour days with eight to ten employees in the "Hairston Woods." They kept the mill supplied with logs on skids for sawing. Men did this work by using their bare hands with no mechanical cutting or logging equipment.

May Victoria Lester was born on January 8, 1913, to George Tilden and Frances Turner Lester. The next year in 1914, George Tilden Lester again moved his company. This time it was for the final time and it was to Jones Creek, another tributary of the Smith River, closer to Martinsville, which gave the company access to the railroad.

Nearly fifty years earlier cavalry under the overall command of George Stoneman led by Brevet Brigadier General William Jackson Palmer fought the cavalry of Confederate James T. Wheeler along the banks of Jones Creek. George Tilden Lester's father George Washington Lester I fought Stoneman as a member of the 10th Virginia Cavalry during the Chancellorsville Campaign of 1863. Two years later part of Stoneman's command visited the future of site Lester Lumber Company.

Lester Lumber Company began to take a "proprietary position" using a special bending and shaping technique for the white oak plow handles produced in droves at the Jones Creek operation. The increase in steam power due to electricity in Martinsville allowed the new process to work. Sawmilling at Figsboro continued with horses and wagons hauling the lumber to Martinsville by horse and wagon until the 1920s.

George and Parker Lester moved into a "Company House" with three bedrooms, a bathroom, living room with furniture made of Michigan Oak including a desk, table, and a clock on the mantel that chimed. There was a kitchen and dining room.

On January 21, 1917, Parker gave birth to twins, Mable and Myrtle, at Jones Creek on Franklin Street in Martinsville. The twins had a double carriage and they woke each other by pulling finger, hair, or each other's toes. Myrtle was a demanding child that required rocking until age five.

On February 3, 1917, Lester Lumber Company made another big step with a capitalization of $50,000 under George Tilden Lester as President. With Vaughan M. Draper served as Secretary, with Nick Prillaman as Treasurer, William Lester, J. A.

Richardson, W. D. Belton, H. J. Turner, and Loury L. Lester as members of the Board of Directors.

As World War One raged all over the world, Woodrow Wilson sent the United States into the "War to end all Wars." On October 20, 1917, George Tilden Lester swore an oath of enlistment in the Virginia Volunteers in Martinsville. Whether this was out of a patriotic calling, it is interesting with a growing family and growing business that "Cap'n Til" was willing to leave it all behind, but at 41 he was too old. He stood five foot eight inches tall with 20/20 eyesight with a chest size of 40 and waist of 34 inches. With dark hair, dark complexion, and brown eyes like his father, the service discharged deeming his business at Martinsville as the reason.

Other Lesters with draft registration cards included Powell Jackson Lester, a farmer, Robert Lester, a farmer was born in 1892, Ainsley Jackson Lester, a farmer and traveling salesman, Loury Lawson Lester, a farmer and lumber, Thomas Oscar Lester, a farmer, John R. Lester, born in 1887 was a traveling salesman and Henry Claybrook Lester born in 1898 was a student at Virginia Polytechnic Institute.

Parker Turner Lester again lived in a new house, but she had bigger plans. A family tradition holds that Parker visited the Richard King Ranch in Texas or more likely saw a photo of the palatial ranch house built in 1915 and she fell in love with the structure. The white brick house looked like a medieval fortress with large curved arches. No doubt Parker Turner Lester told her husband about the house. He did not forget it. Having inherited money from her one armed father, she purchased a lot on Starling Avenue in Martinsville. Tradition holds she hired an architect and had plans drawn up. Sadly, she never saw it built.

After the birth of her twin girls Mable and Myrtle, Parker noticed a lump under her arm. Diagnosed as breast cancer, "Cap'n Til" and Dr. Shackelford took Parker to John Hopkins Hospital near Washington D. C. She had surgery. Grandmother Victoria Waid Lester and her new husband Michael Eggleston Draper along with Drucilla Hurd, who had lived with Victoria for years, came to stay with the children on Jones Creek in Martinsville.

Parker spent three weeks in the hospital. She came home the day before Thanksgiving and was happy to be home. She looked at her twins in their cribs and spent a good night at home. The second day home she complained of fatigue and as night fell George Tilden Lester helped his ailing wife upstairs. Suddenly, he returned downstairs and called for the doctor. Parker had a massive heart attack. Dr. Shackelford arrived and sent to the drugstore for medicine, but it was too late. Parker Turner Lester passed away with her family standing around her bed on November 29, 1917.

The next day they laid her in the dining room. She requested no embalming and her daughter Julia remembered it as one of the coldest days of her life.

Home of: George T. Lester. Figsboro 1913

Parker Turner Lester, first wife of George "Capt'n Till" Lester.

Chapter Eight
Living In A Wedding Cake

Life changed for the Lesters. "We learned the hard side of life." Julia asked Aunt Vickie Turner why God took her mother. Vickie told her that it would be the first thing we will ask the Lord when we get to heaven. "We see through a glass darkly, but when we see Jesus we will understand." Morton and Vickie Turner offered to take May and Julia Lester, but "Cap'n Til" did not break up his family. His daughter said that "Cap'n Til" did not like his sister in law Vickie Turner, who had been against the marriage of Parker and Lester.

It snowed from Thanksgiving to March that year. Every day after walking back and forth to school, Julia remembered breaking ice on a tub on the back porch to wash Mabel and Myrtle's diapers. Julia remembered the house was always cold and Victoria Waid Lester told her son that she would not spend another winter along Jones Creek.

In 1918, George Tilden Lester built his last home on Starling Avenue in Martinsville at a cost of $1,631. The three-story building of white pressed brick and colonnaded porches reminds many of a "frosted wedding cake." Lester described it as "just good old mountaineer architecture," but this author has come to feel that it is something more. Did George T. Lester remember his dead wife's dream? We will never know, but as Parker bought the lot on Starling and family tradition says she was in love with the white brick home at the King Ranch in Texas, it make sense to this author that Lester built a home as a tribute to his late wife.

This author first encountered the "Wedding Cake House" in a book titled *Weird Virginia*: *Your Travel Guide to Virginia's Local Legends and Best Kept Secrets* by authors Jeff Bahr, Troy Taylor, and Lauren Coleman. "We can't say for sure why he did it, but in the early 1900s a man named George 'Cap'n Til' Lester built a three tiered house that looks uncannily like a wedding cake, including festive decorations in its faux 'icing.' Mysteries notwithstanding, the wedding cake house, located at 308 Starling Avenue in Martinsville, is quite a sight. From the magnificent portico featuring six sumptuous arches (in tasty vanilla, we imagine) all the way up to its trademark diagonally oriented third tier, this architectural tidbit may remind married folk of one of two things: the absolute best day of their lives or, perhaps, the worst decision of their lives. Closer examination reveals yet more tasty details, not the least of which is three separate patio areas on the first, second, and third levels. Likely intended for the newlywed phase when sweet nothings were buzzing about like bees in a hive, these open spaces could also pull double duty if the groom wound up in the doghouse and found himself in need of a place to sleep." This book series is a companion for each state to the television series on the A&E and History Channel television networks Weird U. S. hosted by Mark Moran and Mark Sceurman. The article concludes this way. "These days the Wedding Cake House is without a resident bride and groom. We think that's a darn shame. Let's hope a couple of starry-eyed newlyweds will happen along and adopt the place as their own. If that occurs, this bride in particular should feel indebted to ol' Cap'n Lester. After all, she'll get to have her cake and eat it too."

"Cap'n Til" Lester said of the home. "People were building their first indoor bathrooms. But they always tracked them on the outer wall so the pipes were continually freezing up. I figured to beat that by beginning with a three story square in the center of the house to include the basement heating system, bathrooms, and stairway. The walls of this core run straight to the roof." The rooms have five sides. Radiators built into the base of walls and ventilators at the top radiated heat. The house had very plain furniture with two warm bathrooms. There was an icebox, kitchen cabinets and a woodstove. "Cap'n Til" picked out the furniture described as "rough looking" with good metal beds.

There were fourteen main rooms and every room had a door leading to a bathroom. Floors of cherry and walnut felt the heat from coal and later gas heat. The "penthouse" was a sleeping porch.

The white bricks came from a company in Buena Vista, Virginia, made the house "a veritable fortress." Always looking for a deal, "Cap'n Til" bought the bricks for $8 per thousand. The white pressed brick came from a "Special German Kiln." Forty years after construction, Lester thought the same bricks cost $40 per thousand and that the house cost $6,000 to build would be worth five times that in 1957.

The Lesters were not the only ones who came to Starling Avenue in September 1918. Grandma Vickie, Victoria Waid Lester, came to live with them. She brought a rug that looked like a bear and two cows with her. The cows had a shed built for them too. Julia remembered, "Whatever Grandmother Vickie said, Daddy always did." "She was mammy and mammy's authority was certainly law and almost Gospel." Victoria Waid Lester took care of Mable and Drucilla Hurd took care of Myrtle. Julia remembered her grandmother Victoria had a large furniture chest and with a large top, where pies and cakes were kept in the bottom.

During the great influenza epidemic of 1918, a traveling salesman told George Tilden Lester that a grapefruit a day would keep his children safe. He bought crates of grapefruit and made the children eat one every morning. Julia remembered having grapefruit with no sugar that was "green as grass" and "bitter as quinine," but no one got the flu that killed millions worldwide.

Julia Lester, the oldest child, said of her father that he "struggled" without a wife. He put his children to bed and read the bible to them. He "made sure our literature was good and clean." The stress was showing on him as Julia stated that her father never cursed until the death of his first wife.

Living in the "Wedding Cake" house was Mike Draper, Victoria Waid Lester's new husband. He cooked chitterlings. It smelled "worse than a hog pen" and buzzards would roost on the roof drawn by the smell. Julia Lester said it upset her father.

George T. Lester began many important relationships after moving to Martinsville. John D. Bassett founded Bassett Furniture in 1902 and several years later G. T. Lester walked the "muddy crossties" of the Norfolk and Western Railroad to collect a bill. Bassett spotted Lester and invited him into his office to discuss timber and a friendship was born. Bassett often called on Lester to solve mechanical problems. Lester supplied lumber to the Bassett Furniture in the 1920s and 1930s at a time when the Lester Lumber Company needed the business.

In 1916, the lumber processing plant at Figsboro burned. Three years later on November 18, 1919, a fire at Jones Creek destroyed the business that George Tilden Lester had spent years building including all the machinery he developed. The estimated loss was $200,000. Fuel for the fire came from the stockpiling of paint and supplies including a cache of low priced Bolivian and Brazilian linseed oil. The flooding of Jones Creek led to storing the flammable items so closely stored together.

"Cap'n Till" disliked Novembers. He lost Parker in November 1917 and his plant in November 1919. He expressed for years that he was always glad when November passed.

With no insurance and only his good name, good credit and good employees, George Tilden Lester had to start over. "Cap'n Til" told his mother, "Ma, we are paupers again." His friendship with J. D. Bassett and the local banks willingness to extend "unlimited credit," allowed Lester to begin again.

George Washington Lester II, the youngest son of George Tilden Lester, is a movie buff and well aware the line from Star Trek where Mr. Spock speaks of there always being possibilities. George Tilden Lester looked to new possibilities after the fire. He took the opportunity to steer his business in a new direction with a plant for wood materials used in home construction. He built five dry kilns and a wood working shop measured at 160x520 feet.

Hardwood flooring replaced plow handles as the main product. Large barrels for storing and shipping tobacco, "sawed liner," became another product of Lester Lumber Company. Lester got a trial order of 500 liners and soon the other tobacco companies adopted the product. Demand became so great that Lester Lumber Company developed an automatic coiling machine that used boiling water.

Every year "Cap'n Til" paid a dividend on the stock for Lester Lumber Company and he "cursed it." The personality of George Tilden Lester, Sr. is the thing of legend and probably exaggerated over time to make him bigger than life. Feuds and gunfire are a part of the fabric of Southern life. The media blew the Hatfields and McCoys out of proportion while the shootout at the Carroll County Court House in Hillsville has regional appeal. Martinsville and Henry County nearly had a similar event that certainly would have changed the direction of the Lester Lumber Company. Whether apocryphal or not the family tradition is that Walter Wade Lester, the oldest son of George Washington Lester was put on trial for making whiskey that killed a man. The courtroom was tense as the verdict was about to come down. William A. Lester had pearl handled revolvers, but beside him was his relative George Tilden "Cap'n Til" Lester himself armed. One imagines if the jury foreman read a guilty verdict that the Lesters would join the Allens of Carroll County in infamy, prison or the electric chair. Luckily, the jury found Walter Lester not guilty and the potential gunfire did not occur.

Henry Clay Lester Tobacco Factory in Figsboro in 1886.

Chapter Nine
A Swimming Pool and a Castle

A judge holding court in the old Martinsville Henry County Courthouse was presiding over a case in the 1950s. During the intermission between two cases, someone commented on the safety of the building as the blasting and shaking of the earth was causing much distraction during the session. The judge commenting on the destruction of the Liberty Heights Swimming Pool commented on the "sound of progress" sat back in his chair and called for the next case. One change is obvious to anyone studying the business career of the man who was George Tilden Lester, Sr. He "tired of wood buildings burning and wanted to build more permanently." This not only became a trademark for Lester in his business, but in his future home on Starling Avenue and even the swimming pool he became famous for. Tradition says that he got the nickname "Cap'n Til" due to his knack for getting the most for his money.

If you are in the lumber business you know that fire is the enemy. The cliché says that the enemy of my enemy is my friend. The enemy of fire is water. George Tilden Lester made friends with water and gave the community he lived in a place for recreation that became a landmark.

Early in the 1920's, the local Kiwanis Club asked Lester for a contribution to build a new local swimming pool. Lester suggested turning his fire reservoir into a citywide recreation center. Liberty Heights Swimming Pool was born. Lester Lumber Company pumped two million gallons of water to the reservoir for the fire protection up the hill from Jones Creek in the hopes that if needed, the gravity fed system would suppress any fires. There were fires that needed the services of the system, but there were many more great times had by those who used the pool.

Liberty Heights was once over two hundred feet higher than it is today. "Cap'n Til" used mules, horses, and drag pans to cut down the mountain gaining the name of "Mountain Mover." An airport and swimming pool resulted from the leveling of the mountaintop.

Low cement walls divided the pool into various depths. The pools circumference was 1,000 feet. It cost $100,000 to build over sixteen months with 25,000 one hundred pound bags of concrete creating a pool of 260x130 feet. The massive building had locker and dressing rooms in the lower levels. The three tiers of circular concrete looked like a spider web, "one of the strongest structures in nature" Lester noted. For thirty-one years, the pool was a great place for a good time and very few who used it knew that they were swimming and diving in a fire suppression system for a lumber plant. Lester pumped water 200 feet from Jones Creek at a rate of 360,000 gallons every hour. Fourteen-inch pipes from Fort Sumter, South Carolina, carried the water up from Jones Creek at 6,000 gallons per minute. Twelve-inch pipe carried water down to the Lester Lumber Company to put out fires. The aeration/filtration systems cost $50,000 to build. There were five filters, which all the water went through every six hours keeping algae from growing in the pool. When water levels grew low, a flag signal started the pumping from Jones Creek to the swimming pool 200 hundred feet above. A signal to swimmers beeped on a horn when the fire system was in operation.

On July 4, 1926, one hundred years to the day Thomas Jefferson died, the Liberty Heights Swimming Pool opened. Looking like a "Roman Coliseum," it was not just a summer facility, but an ice rink in the winter and an open-air market with individual stalls.

Some ladies received free passes, brass pins, and they became pool mothers, who watched over the younger children. These same mothers kept their children at home during Polio scares in the 1940s and 1950s, but they came back to Liberty Heights Swimming Pool.

The pool held 2,000 swimmers, who saw the sign "Cap'n Til" Lester, the Primitive Baptist, placed there saying, "Do Unto

Others As You Would Have Them Do Unto You." There were three levels with an eighteen-inch deep "baby pool," proceeding over the wall to four feet and the inner section that sloped to twelve feet with a diving board in the center. The diving platform was three tiered with a twenty-foot high dive. Originally, there were only two sections, but when inexperienced swimmers went over the wall and began to slide down into the deeper sections, Lester constructed a second wall. Admission was fifty cents for swimmers and twenty-five cents for children and "spectators." Swimmers got locker keys they attached to their suits with safety pins.

    Among the Lesters, Myrtle was a great swimmer often winning the July 4th watermelon race. Watermelons thrown into the pool were for "whoever could wrestle them out got to keep them." G. T. Lester, Jr. was the first lifeguard. George Washington Lester II nearly drowned once in his father's pool. The youngest son of "Cap'n Til" tells how he resigned himself to death and a warm feeling came over him. Suddenly, his older brother jerked him out of the deep water by the hair of the head. Another swimmer said he learned to swim at Liberty Heights "not from instruction, but from ridicule." One swimmer said there was so much chlorine that a blonde turned her hair green.

There was a dance hall with mirrors between the windows to give the room a more spacious appearance. 500 couples danced at a time on the oak floors of the pavilion, which measured 200x83 feet. When not dancing, roller skaters used the facility.

In 1931, wind blew off the roof. Richard P. Gravely, Jr. served as a lifeguard from 1930 until 1932. He thought a tornado tore the roof of the building. Workers tore up the oak floorboards and turned it into a sunbathing deck. Gravely said that before construction of the middle ring that he could see keys and coins at the bottom of the pool, but the new ring affected the flow. About this time, "Cap'n Til" told Edwin "Podner" Penn that the "pool paid for itself last night." The fire suppression system put out a fire at the Lester Lumber Company.

Famous and average people came to Liberty Heights. Country singer Roy Acuff performed on the dance floor and Governor Harry Byrd flew into the airport to announce his candidacy for Governor of Virginia. Organizers conducted local beauty pageants at the swimming pool and there were even slot machines at the lunch counter.

A caretaker named Ben Jones lived at the Liberty Heights Swimming Pool. Jones could not do strenuous work because of a chlorine gas attack he suffered through during World War One. He lived there year round in three rooms including a kitchen and bathroom even when the pool was not open.

Ever the mechanical innovator, "Cap'n Til's" swimming pool called the "South's finest aquatic emporium" was an engineering marvel. The New York City Department of Public Works studied the design.

In 1957, the city annexed the land of Lester Lumber Company, so city water now flowed into the fire suppression system at the lumber plant. This coincided with the end of segregation and as African-Americans did not swim in the Liberty Heights Pool, the facility closed, the same year the U. S. Supreme Court ruled segregation illegal. Thirty years later demolition began. The site is now the home of the Liberty Fair Mall, another of the civic-minded project of the Lesters. Estimated at 2 ½ million pounds of concrete it took six months to bring down the structure.

"Cap'n Til" was a man of his concrete and railroads as one writer noted that every structure he built after the fire at Lester Lumber Company in 1919 had both. The swimming pool had two short tracks with a winch to pull carts of food and other materials from the ground level to the pavilion level. Among those foods fondly remembered were frozen Milky Way bars.

When the bulldozers began to tear down the Liberty Heights Swimming Pool in 1987, there is a video of George W.

Lester II walking around the building with a camera crew. He summed it up this way. "The first time I ever saw it I thought it was the biggest building I ever saw. It had the most water, the most people, and the most fun. I don't remember trips to and from the swimming pool, but I remember the times spent here. I remember the laughter of people, carefree attitudes, and the release of vacation. It was the time of adjustment in the 1940s after the war. The pool was enjoying life with simple things such as sunshine, water, warmth and relaxing together. I learned to swim here and formed lifelong friendships here. It seemed like an eternal, a perpetual place. It was a monument to Henry County as people from Roanoke, Danville, and even Winston-Salem came here to swim. Liberty Heights will only be in people's hearts now."

After turning over Lester Lumber Company to George Tilden Lester, Jr. in 1939, "Cap'n Til" devoted his life to moving mountains, literally tearing them down with earth moving equipment. At one time he had thirteen pands, heavy earth moving machines. He started with mules and manual labor and ended with bulldozers.

Years later while cutting out the right of way for the Kings Mountain Road, "Cap'n Til" personally set a dynamite charge to dislodge some rock. He moved his men back and lit the fuse and walked back "calmly" to his "battered old automobile coupe." He stepped on the starter and nothing happened. After several attempts Lester after letting out "one of the oaths for which he was famous" reportedly said to his vehicle "Well, you can sit here and get blown up, but I'm getting the hell out of here." When he returned to his car covered in rock, he discovered that he had not turned on the ignition. At this point the "Old Cap'n" cussed himself.

The editor of the Martinsville Bulletin K. L. Thompson told a story about Lester's vision. While both men waited in the Herbert Kidd Barbershop on a Saturday night, which stayed open late then because people like Lester worked six days a week. Thompson asked Lester which direction from Martinsville the greatest growth would come in the future. Lester replied that he thought Collinsville would. He said, "The territory is close to Bassett, Fieldale, and Martinsville. Besides there is an ample supply of water and most of the land is flat." He felt that when the "old, torturous route by way of Koehler" would give way to a modern road, today's business 220.

Continuing his believe that fire is the enemy and concrete will not burn, George T. Lester, Sr. started a plant at Koehler, near Fieldale, along the Smith River that made use of the river sand and gravel to make concrete block. The three-story plant "resembled a vast, rambling Rhineland castle," but took advantage of literally sitting on the banks of the Smith River and Beaver Creek as the latter emptied into the former. The process involved gravel dredged and pumped into the building, screened, washed, graded and carried on conveyors to storage hoppers. The plant cast concrete into "Superoc" blocks that were "acoustical material of moist Portland Cement and a special grade of slag." "Heavy Tamping" Machines pressed the blocks and placed them on pallets mounted along a circumference on subterranean turntables. In spite of his best efforts fire reared its ugly head on May 1, 1944, and destroyed the machinery of the plant. G. T. Lester, Jr. estimated the damage at $8,000. George Oakley said the fire began in an electrical switch operating a belt pulley. Along with the fire, the building of the Philpot Dam on the Smith River cut off the sand supply from the flooding river. While the large concrete structure still sits on the banks of both watercourses, today it is a warehouse.

    Koehler began in 1898 named for Mr. Koehler's lumber company. George T. Lester, Sr. bought land along the Smith River in 1919. In 1921, the first paved road in Henry County came through Koehler on its way from Martinsville to Rocky Mount, Virginia. Known as the Wray Route, Waller Road for the nearby ford at Waller's now Fieldale, National Highway #3, and Route 57, the "subway" traveled under the railroad. Five years later, the Danville and Western Railroad built a siding.

Told he could not place a building on the banks of the Smith River due to the size and weight, "Cap'n Til" built his "Rhineland Castle" anyway to produce his sand and gravel concrete blocks. Year later the Martinsville Jaycees rented the building during Halloween as a "Haunted House."

Lester's "Castle" in Koehler in 2009.

Chapter Ten
Cap'n Til and Lottie

Meeting your new husband's family is always stressful for a young woman, but to meet the brother of your new husband's first wife and his wife is even more of an uncomfortable situation. Lottie Floy Shelton Lester baked a chocolate cake for Morton and Vickie Turner. Before she could serve it the twin daughters of Parker Turner Lester, Mable and Myrtle age three discovered the prize dessert and ate all the icing off the sides of the cake.

Like many things in her new life, Lottie did not complain, she just "worked with us," said her stepdaughter Julia, who was only eight years younger than Lottie. Others such as Drucilla Hurd, who came to live with Victoria Waid Lester Draper, did not like Lottie, but Julia Lester said her new stepmother "weathered the storm with her calmness."

Lottie Floy Shelton was born on December 31, 1898, to Ferdinand Smith (1874-1957) and Vinecie Stone Shelton (1877-1945). Her father moved often. This wanderlust took him from where he was born in Franklin County on Mill Creek to the Blackberry section of Henry County where he farmed. He moved to Henry, Virginia, where he operated a distillery. Then he moved to Reed Creek where he bought a farm. In 1909, he moved to

Roanoke County near the airport and spent the next six years there livestock farming. Three years in Botetourt County came next. In 1918, he moved south of Roanoke near Cave Spring where Lottie completed her senior year of high school.

Lottie went to school in Roanoke County and Asbury. She finished at Salem High School, where she played center on a nine girl basketball team. One of her favorite subjects was history.

Lottie's siblings included Dombey Jackson Shelton born in 1900, Harmon David Shelton born in 1904, Roy Tilden Shelton in 1906, Ferdinand Taft Shelton in 1908, Steven Turner Shelton born in 1910, and James Calvin Shelton born in 1913. Lottie's mother was the child of Andrew Jackson and Cassie Elizabeth Stone. Her father, Ferdinand was the child of Harmon David and Susan Ann Smith.

After high school, Lottie got a Teaching Certificate from Radford Normal School, now Radford University. In July 1920, she stood five foot eight inches tall and weighed 145 pounds when she taught in the Roanoke County schools. She taught at Deyerle and Cave Springs and took classes in the summer before receiving her teaching certificate on August 16, 1920.

George Tilden Lester, Sr. met Lottie Floy Shelton at Camp Branch Primitive Baptist Church. After a "quick courtship," they were married on September 20, 1920. Stepmother and stepdaughter bonded. Julia Lester said that Lottie made sure she had nice clothes and being a teacher she helped with Julia's algebra.

Many visitors came to the "Cake House" on Starling Avenue. Mike and Victoria Waid Lester Draper had guests and held "signings." Mike's sister came to visit with her seven children. One which had a "bad heart," which concerned Lottie Lester.

Lottie's parents visited and stayed in Julia's room, who tried to keep the room clean for them. Myrtle and Mabel continued their antics that horrified their new stepmother. Julia said that Myrtle would "act like a monkey" when guests were present.

Julia Lester continued her visits to her mother's family in Roanoke. "Cap'n Til" bought her a completely new wardrobe. A Mrs. Holt labeled the outfits on the shoulders for the different occasions such as dinner with Mary and Curtis Turner.

In 1921, Lottie had twins who died at birth on November 21. A daughter Floy Christine was born on September 24, 1922. Two years later two twins, Angel and Noble were born on February 11, 1924, but sadly only lived a four months. The following year 1925 Doris Angeline "Jack" Lester was born on June 12. At age two she developed "trouble with her bones." Julia remembered milking the cow every day to get her milk.

Marrying the daughter of your boss is daunting for most men, but not George Dillard Oakley (1901-1983). Many of his co-workers did not think Oakley would survive his first date with the oldest daughter of George Tilden "Cap'n Til" Lester, Julia. During a picnic at Cliff Springs Julia Lester saw George Dillard Oakley. She said for years he brought things to the "Wedding Cake House," but she said he "never paid any attention to me at all." At the picnic he asked Julia to walk down the hill to see some carvings on some trees. While Julia was concerned about ruining her shoes, Dillard had another agenda and asked her out for Saturday night. One can imagine the look on George T. Lester's face when his daughter descended the stairs dressed in her "flapper clothes" for her date with Oakley. The Captain told Julia that Oakley had a girlfriend on Water Street, but that did not deter Julia. Oakley took her to meet his mother and took her to family reunions.

When George D. Oakley married Julia Lester, Lottie gave them a silver set as a wedding present when she did not own one herself. Married on December 29, 1926, this union produced Sally Parker Oakley, who married Garland Dwight Burch. Next born was George D. Oakley, Jr., who married first Nancy Ann Jones and then Janet Lewis. John Benjamin Oakley was the next child born to Julia and G. D. Oakley. John married Julia Angeline

Riddle. Julia Lester was the next daughter and she married Kenneth Wayne. The last son Robert James Oakley married Peggy Williams.

Lottie got a Roanoke architect named Wood to help build a house for the Oakleys on Mulberry with "Cap'n Til's" help. Described as a "Normandy Bungalow," the house has two floors below ground. They moved in during 1932. This was the house "where children came" because their mothers did not want the mess. It was a place cookies baked and Easter eggs found their dye. One day Julia looked up to see a pony in her house because one of the neighbor boys wanted her to see it.

Aunt Sara Draper moved into the "Wedding Cake House" with the family for years. Uncle Oscar Lester stayed for three months and Aunt Pearl Lester for over a year. Draper had arthritis so bad that the family turned her in bed sheets. There were as many as nineteen people living on Starling Avenue at one time. May and George T. Jr. invited guests for Sunday lunch. With so many people living in the house on Starling Avenue, they had to eat meals in shifts. When Drucilla Hurd became disabled, Lottie picked up the workload.

The Lesters hand churned butter. They had flat irons heated on the wood cook stove. Lottie and Sarah Darper made dresses for the girls out of 36 yards of lace. There was great joy when Lester purchased an electric iron. There were two laundry tubs where the family scrubbed clothes on an oak board. Julia remembered washing and starching while Lottie rinsed and hung the clothes when bad weather kept their "washer woman" from coming.

Mabel and Myrtle continued to be a special issue. When they got angry they dumped their clothes into the floor of the hall not their rooms. They loved to play on the second floor roof, where they got "black as tar babies." The twins skated on the front porch when not falling out of swings onto their heads. The girls went to Buena Vista College with "real nice clothes." Myrtle fell in love with a neighbor, Starkey Poteat, and stood in the yard for hours talking to him through rain, snow, and even hail. Myrtle later dated Jesse Snyder, who "could tell more funny jokes than anyone I have ever met."

The family visited Mary Waid on the Pigg River, the present day Waid Recreation Area in Franklin County. Myrtle's boyfriend there had the ironic name of Bud Robertson, but not the Alumni Distinguished Professor of History at Virginia Tech. Myrtle attended National Business College in Roanoke, but came home every weekend. She worked there after school because "she looked able." Myrtle's future husband was selling tobacco in Martinsville and lived with the Lesters for a short time. They built a house at Figsboro and lived there for two years before moving to South Carolina where they "were happy on the farm."

Living in the "Wedding Cake House" raising the children of Parker Turner Lester and her own presented special issues for Lottie Shelton Lester. Julia quoted her father once as saying, "How wonderful our mother (Parker) was and none of his children would come to be like her." Julia said that she thought Myrtle reached that "high plane," but that Lottie always worried about her. George T. Lester, Sr. seldom spoke of his first wife in front of his second wife as a sign of respect. Julia said, "We were blessed with two wonderful mothers." "Lottie did everything she could for us."

In 1927, Lottie gave birth to a son, Darwin Demosthenes "Bo" on October 4. Described as "the most meticulous male I ever met," Julia said when her child Sally was born that Bo looked after her and did not like her to get dirty.

In May 1932, May Victoria Lester visited Pilot Mountain in North Carolina. She came back and got sick. She died of pneumonia "For the soul to be absent from the body that the person was ever present with the Lord." "We are all so blessed that God gave her to us as long as He did."

On February 12, 1936, Tilden Jackson Lester was born to Lottie and George Tilden Lester, Sr. George Washington Lester II was born in 1939, the last child of "Cap'n Til" and Lottie, on April 4.

Myrtle Morton Lester married Robert Bell. Her twin sister Mabel Parker Lester married Leslie Wells.

Lester Lumber Company continued to grow during the Great Depression. G. T. Lester, Jr. took over day-to-day operations of Lester Lumber Company in 1939 and held that position for the next twenty-five years. World War Two brought contracts for barracks and package houses for export to Russia. These "Model-T" of pre-fabricated dwellings were tough to manufacturer due to a lack of machinery and tools, so Lester Lumber Company built its own machinery and developed procedures still in use today in pre-fabricated construction.

During World War Two, Lottie had a Victory Garden. Over the years she was active in the Greenwood Garden Club and won awards for "Horticultural Achievement." She volunteered for the American Red Cross and attended church at Martinsville Primitive Baptist Church. Lottie lost her mother in 1945 and Ferdinand Shelton came to live with his daughter on Starling Avenue in Martinsville until his death in 1957.

Other residents on Starling Avenue included animals. Bo had a raccoon named Jaboney, who got out of his cage frequently and came into the house. He got under Grandfather Shelton's bed.

One day he ventured into "Cap'n Til's" bed and pulled up the covers.

In September 1947, "Bo" lost his life in a freak accident. While visiting a young lady, Charlotte Westervelt, a student at Westhampton College in Richmond, Darwin Demosthenes "Bo" Lester was driving his date and another couple Miss Jett Carter and Irving M. Graves III, a student at Randolph-Macon College back to campus from the Westhampton Theatre. At approximately 11:50 p.m., a gun, a 22-caliber pistol, fell from the sun visor and struck the steering wheel shooting Lester in the head just over his left eye. "Bo" survived for ten hours. He had just entered North Carolina State University as a freshman after eighteen months in the U. S. Army in the Pacific Theater. That summer he was a lifeguard at Liberty Heights Swimming Pool. He graduated from Martinsville High School where he was a great athlete playing football and gymnastics. John Redd Smith, who was dating sister "Jack" at the time, encountered "Cap'n Til," who told him, "Brother Smith, I've lost my boy." Smith stated to this author that it "tore him up" to see Lester so obviously distraught over the death of his son.

After the war Lester Lumber Company returned to hardwood flooring and building materials. In 1949, Lester Home Center on Liberty Street came into being along with the Wholesale Supply Service. In the 1950s, a modern band sawmill made for more efficient timber manufacturing with minimum waste. In 1957, a fire destroyed the four-story retail store, materials warehouse, and office on Franklin Street.

Stories about George Tilden Lester, Sr. "Cap'n Till" abound. One from his oldest son, G. T. Lester, makes a point about his frugality. The company got the contract to pave the roads in Martinsville, but the solid rubber welded to the wheel rims of the tires wore off hauling the cement. It was too expensive to buy rubber tires, so Lester rode the rims. This jarred the streets and buildings so bad the town sent notice to Lester to cease. To make any money on the contract Lester could not buy tires, so he ignored the officials and jarred them until the contract was complete.

"Cap'n Til" did not put up with laziness or wasting money. Once when as a young man G. T. Lester, Jr. had admired his sister Julia's shoes and talked the "Cap'n" into buying him a pair. When he wore the shoes to school he soon found that the other boys were not impressed. The Richardson and Belton boys ran interference, but he had a choice of fighting or running. G. T. Lester, Jr. did not tell his father, but Grandmother Vickie did. "Cap'n Till's" response. "Wear those shoes!" G. T. Lester, Jr. did not think the shoes would ever wear out.

Not to belabor the point, but Lester studied a problem in his mind developing a three dimensional view of the solution focusing on the design with his brain. If anyone asked for a written design, Lester would "fish an old envelope from his pocket and draw a rough, impatient sketch." George Tilden Lester continued his gift for invention. He devised a steam boiler to make the Jones Creek plant self-sufficient for electricity by burning waste from the lumber mill. No black smoke or air pollution came from the plant and this devise is only second of his inventions patented. A copy of this patent filed in 1948 is also at the end of this book.

In 1964, at age 88 George Tilden "Cap'n Til" Lester retired as Chairman of the Board of the Lester Lumber Company. One local author wrote of him that he "began early in his career to acquire substantial acreage in timber both in Virginia and neighboring North Carolina. These holdings not only provided raw material for his lumber business, but enabled him to exercise an inborn love for moving earth."

William Blake wrote, "Great things are done when men and mountains meet." George Tilden "Cap'n Til" Lester, Sr. was born the year Reconstruction ended after the Civil War. He lived to see men landing on the moon. He started "below the bottom rung of the ladder" with his adult life beginning shackled with the debts of his father and to his credit, he paid them and built his own business through perseverance suffering repeated professional and personal tragedy. He started with plug tobacco and built a lumber business that started making plow handles diversified into hardwood flooring, millwork, and a building supply company. There is much to admire in the life of such a man. He was bigger than life in many ways, but he was a human being who worked extremely hard and expected it of those around especially his sons and male relatives.

One writer described George Tilden "Cap'n Til" Lester at age 93 as "the man who has become a legend in Virginia's lumber industry still takes an active interest in the affairs of his business and his community." He was a man who "didn't hesitate to slice off the top of a mountain to build an airport" or a swimming pool. George Tilden Lester, the hard shell Baptist and hardnosed businessman went to his maker on March 20, 1973. He rests today in Martinsville's Oakwood Cemetery surrounded by his wives and family as he always was. The Martinsville Bulletin wrote, "No man in the history of Martinsville and Henry County has done more to change the landscape of our area."

Chapter Eleven
Flying High

George Tilden Lester Jr. served as the second President of Lester Lumber Company from 1939 until 1964. G. T. Lester, Jr. developed a keen interest in planes and flying. He got his first plane in 1935, a 37 horsepower cub. He paid an instructor $4.00 an hour for training and with the 400 pounds of weight with instructor and student off into the wild blue yonder they went. They got about 500 feet above the ground and the instructor let go of the controls. G. T. Lester, Jr. continued instruction in Lynchburg, Danville, and Roanoke.

In 1938, he bought his first airplane for $2,200 and went to Cincinnati, Ohio, to pick it up. He said he flew back "by the iron compass" following the railroad tracks from Ohio. The plane was the first airplane in Henry County and Martinsville, but it burned up in a hangar fire in the 1940s. G. T. Lester, Jr. barn stormed with a parachute jumper named Stinky Davis, who apparently did not bathe often. They flew from the Bleak Hill in Franklin County, Laurel Fork near Highway 58 along the Patrick/Carroll County border and as far south as Lenoir, North Carolina.

G. T. Lester, Jr. married Annie Sue Walker Waid on July 6, 1932. Annie descended from the Waids of Franklin County already covered earlier in this book.

His son, Morton Waid Lester born in 1933. and like his father has a great love of aviation. He soloed at age ten. He used seat cushions taken from other parked planes and piled them up to get high enough to see out and reach the pedals. He served in Korea in the Signal Corps stationed at Fort Gordon, Georgia, where he flew his plane. Morton attended Virginia Tech and flew his plane back and forth to Blacksburg. If he had no afternoon class he often flew home to have lunch with his father. Being a true Hokie, Lester took part in aggravating the rival of his day the Keydets of the Virginia Military Institute. A quick flight to Lexington with a planned arrival during the evening dress parade of the Keydets resulted in paper bags full of flour arriving with on the parade ground and onto the men in line. Lester served on the 1955 Ring Committee charged with the design of that class's ring. Each class has a unique ring including this author and many others who call the Orange and Maroon an alma mater. Morton is a member of the Old Guard, a special alumni designation given to those in the Alumni Association who have reached the fiftieth anniversary of their graduation. Today, when you visit Morton

Lester just behind him you can see the Virginia Tech class ring he helped to design and the certificate for the Old Guard.

Morton worked at Lester Lumber Company before establishing his own company, Lester Corporation, as a building contractor developing homes and apartments. He collects and restores classic airplanes keeping a hangar at Blue Ridge Airport at Spencer as a museum. He donated over a "dozen" airplanes to museums. For twenty-three years he served on the Blue Ridge Airport Authority and the Virginia Aviation Board for a decade. He was involved with the development of the Virginia Aviation Museum in Richmond. In 2001, he gave a vintage World War Two airplane to the D-Day Memorial in nearby Bedford, Virginia.

Lester collected propellers from vintage aircraft and over 300 documentary films. He donated much of this material to the Experimental Aircraft Association Airventure Museum in Oshkosh, Wisconsin. This museum with 200 airplanes is the world's largest private air museum.   Continuing his interest in aviation well into his seventh decade, Morton says, "Every now and then, I have to go up and get some fresh air." The fresh air nearly cost this Lester his life twice in 1973. On June 13, 1973, flying from Martinsville to Tullahoma, Tennessee with two passengers, Morton noted that on this Friday the 13th that the engine was running very smooth at 10,500 feet over the Smoky

Mountains. At that moment, the engine quit and descending at 1,000 feet per minute, Morton had to find a spot to land. He saw a small uphill clearing and nearly got safely on the ground until his right wing clipped a tree. The resulting accident caused two crushed vertebrae and a damaged disk with months of recovery time in a back brace. Thirty days before a broken propeller forced a landing at an army base.

The Lester Lumber Company and the Lester Family have long been civic minded concerned about the well-being of Henry County and Martinsville. Civic development and stimulating the growth of commerce in Martinsville and Henry County were priorities for the family going back several generations.

When fire destroyed two tobacco warehouses in the 1950s, Lester Lumber Company, continuing the trend started by "Cap'n Till" after the 1917 fire, built two concrete and steel warehouses, one fronting Liberty Street and one fronting Franklin Street.

The Lesters built the first airport in Henry County by grading the mountain off Liberty Street. G. T. Lester, Jr. "convinced his father to shave off another mountain top." Lester Lumber Company leased space privately owned aircraft and hanger space. The planes flew over the vast timber holdings of the company. H. K. Saunders from Maiden, North Carolina, came to work at W. M. Bassett Furniture in 1940. He doubled as "grease monkey" at the Lester Airport. G. T. Lester, Jr. taught him to fly. He stayed there for about five years. Of four managers of the Lester Airport, three became commercial pilots and one, Saunders, became Vice-President of Piedmont Airlines. After construction of the airport at Spencer, George Tilden Lester, Sr. gave the right of way to Martinsville for Liberty Street.

During World War Two, the need for an "endless supply" of lumber caused the company to start acquiring land. In 1948, 15 million board feet of lumber and 200 employees produced hardwood flooring, millwork, cement blocks, and building materials.

Over the years Lester Lumber Company gave millions of dollars of land away for civic purposes. The Kings Mountain Road connecting Route 108 to Highway 220 at Collinsville was a short cut for hauling material to Roanoke. "Cap'n Til" loved moving dirt himself and became known as the "Mountain Mover." The company donated all company owned sewer, water, and power easements to the city and the county. Grading all or part of Fairy Street, Watt Street, Northside Drive, and Armory Road were gifts of Lester Lumber Company to the City of Martinsville.

In the 1950s, Lester Lumber Company sold 250 acres of the Beaver Creek Reservoir below original cost for $6,900 along with land for Figsboro Elementary School and Martinsville High

School. In 1954, Lester Lumber Company offered 15 acres on Beaver Creek for a reservoir three miles north of Martinsville. Previously, the company gave six acres already for a picnic site. The city had to build $1,500 for roads and Lester Lumber Company built a parallel road. The 1960s saw 25 acres for Martinsville General Hospital.

    The Martinsville Bulletin of November 24, 1954, said of "Cap'n Til has again demonstrated the intense pride he shows in the ultimate development of every project in which he takes an interest. Mr. Lester is that sort of rugged and visionary individual who can go to the top of a hill and see things far in the future. This is not the first time he had taken a bulldozer or so, a dirt loader and a motor grader by the throttle and carved out something that became more practical both in appearance and in reality with the displacement of each yard of dirt or stone."

    The development of what is today Commonwealth Boulevard began in November 1950 when Lester Lumber Company offered land valued at $217,000 for a right of way for a proposed bypass north of town. For this the city had to within eight years spend $30,000 in grading including a bridge across the Danville and Western Railroad across Fairy Street. This one hundred foot right of way linked four highways leaving present day business 220 at Lester Lumber Company traveling east along

Jones Creek to Liberty Street, then south to the service station still there today, then east of the Lester Lumber Company on Franklin Street, paralleling the railroad emerging near Fairy Street at the intersections of Routes 57 and 58.

In April 1957, a fire destroyed the Lester Lumber Office in downtown Martinsville on Franklin Street. From his home on Starling Avenue "Cap'n Till" watched "the angry glow in the sky clear across town" wondering if the wind would blow it his way. Lester's business endured four separate fires.

In 1960, Lester Lumber Company expanded moving a hardwood flooring plant from Winchester, Kentucky, to Martinsville. The company added a new shop, dry kiln facility and raw lumber storage space and 150 employees.

From 1963-64, a remodeled retail building became a division of the Lester Lumber Company and Wholesale Supply Service that is today the 9,000 item Lester Home Center. In 1969, the office moved to Franklin Street adjacent to the Home Center.

In the 1960s, the Lester Lumber Company owned 25,000 acres of Virginia land in Henry, Franklin, Pittsylvania and Halifax Counties and Rockingham County, North Carolina. Hardwoods of Oak and Poplar (20% from Lester land and 80% from farmers and contract logging) continued to be the source of products for the company.

The sawmill product was air dried on metal trucks for three months of air-drying. Workers then transferred the oak to preheating kilns, the steam heated in dry kilns before cooling the oak for twenty-four hours before the manufacturing process in to random lengths of strip flooring. Other lumber became surrey stakes, shoe molding, step treads, and matting sticks delivered via a fleet of trucks in the eastern and southern United States.

George T. Lester, Jr. died on September 30, 1993, and rests today in Roselawn Cemetery. For thirty-five years he guided the Lester Lumber Company. In 1981, the Virginia Aviation Hall of Fame inducted him. He was a "Charter Member" of the Martinsville Rotary Club and was a deacon in the First Baptist Church. Anne Waid Lester preceded him in death on February 23, 1986. He left a daughter Becky Stone, G. T. Lester III and the aforementioned Morton W. Lester.

Chapter Twelve
Lottie's children

Lottie Floy Shelton Lester moved out of the "Wedding Cake House" on Starling Avenue and into 205 Cornerstone Apartments after "Cap'n Til's" death. Julia Lester said, "Mother could have stayed there, but she didn't want to. No one wanted to live there so we decided to sell." John Jacob Astor Sanders purchased the home. Lottie traveled the world going to Hawaii, England, and Arizona. She kept a dark green Lincoln parked outside her apartment so someone could drive her in an emergency even though she drove herself until 1983. She passed away on February 15, 1990 leaving a legacy as a mother and stepmother. At the time her death, Lottie Floy Shelton Lester had thirty grandchildren, thirty-nine great-grandchildren and one great-great-grandchild. One of her granddaughters said of her, "Granny was the most hardworking, giving, considerate person I have known. I strive to be like her." A grandson of Parker Turner Lester wrote in 1990 about Lottie, "her real legacy to me was in her care for us when were growing up. I'll never forget the memories of 'the House.' Granny was always giving to Granddaddy, to the many guests that she enjoyed, to my mother, and to me. She taught me how to care."

Her stepdaughter Julia Lester Oakley recalled a final meeting with the woman who called her "sister." Lottie pulled Julia close to her and said, "Isn't it good that we've worn out instead of rusting out." Julia said, "She always was beautiful."

Christine Lester married Richard Blythe Sowdon.

Doris Angeline "Jack" Lester married Charles Gilbert Wiswall of Wilmington, Delaware, on October 25, 1949. On May 15, 1983, "Cap'n Til's" grandson visited the White House. John Wiswall, son of Cap'n Til's daughter "Jack," developed Juvenile Rheumatoid Arthritis at age 18 months. By 1983 unable to walk without assistance he was Arthritis Poster Person. On April 11, John and his parents visited the Oval Office and met with Chairperson of the Arthritis Foundation and actress Victoria Principal and another former actor, the forty-fourth President of the United States Ronald Wilson Reagan.

In October 1981, Fire again hit Lester Lumber Company destroying the company's compartment storage area, sawmill, and machine areas including pallet production and planer dimension department. The four-hour fire damaged an estimated $500,000 worth of property, but unlike in 1919 Lester Lumber Company had insurance this time. Repairmen disconnected the fire sprinkler system to repair the roof of the building and sparks from a welding torch started the fire. One hundred and twenty-five fire fighters responded and used over 750,000 gallons of water before bringing the blaze under control including water from the Liberty Heights Swimming Pool.

Tilden J. Lester was a graduate of North Carolina State University in 1955 with a Bachelor's Degree in Forest Products Manufacturing. He served as a 2nd Lieutenant in the U. S. Army Corps of Engineers spending eighteen months in Germany. Tilden served as President and Treasurer of Lester Lumber Company beginning in 1964 with George Washington Lester II as Executive Vice-President and Assistant Treasurer. The company funded a pension plan for the employees along with a profit sharing began in 1966 during his tenure.

In 1968, Lester Lumber Company bought a controlling interest in American Standard Homes Corporation for construction of pre-fabricated "home packages." Tilden J. Lester took over management of the company in 1971 retiring as President of the Lester Group in 1982 Tilden married Marlene Saunders Lester and had sons Darwin Demosthenes Lester and James Arnold Lester. Both sons worked for Lester Lumber Company from the time they were thirteen. They pulled lumber of the "chain" at the lumberyard and loaded houses on trucks at American Standard.

American Standard split off from the Lester Group in 1982. Tilden served as Chairman and CEO of American Standard Homes until his retirement on January 5, 1990. Tilden Jackson Lester passed away on January 5, 1991.

His son Jamie returned in 1987 expecting a job as assistant plant manager and instead found himself working as a line leader in the Wall Department of the manufacturing facility at five dollars an hour. Having graduated from Martinsville High School and Virginia Tech in 1986, Jamie received an MBA from Wake Forest in 1993. Four months of working on the line got this Lester a job as Assistant Plant Manager.

The Lesters sold American Standard in January 1990. Six years later the company filed for Chapter 11 bankruptcy. Having an "emotional attachment" to the company Jamie Lester filed a competing reorganizational plan with the bankruptcy judge feeling that, "If I didn't at least try, I would regret it for the rest of my life." After a year of litigation, when the management team that bankrupted the company tried to continue with the company, the judge chose Lester on March 4, 1997. In 2003, he launched an owner builder program driven by the company's website that was generating over 100 leads a month two years later and 1,200 a month in 2006. The website offered 10,000 standard home plans for custom home design services and 100% contraction financing with a database of 40,000 subcontractors. In 2008, American

Standard again filed for bankruptcy with the down turn of the economy.

In 1966, automation came to the 160 employee Lester Lumber plant. By 1970, flooring was only 25% of factory output. Supplying furniture plants became a prominent role for the Lester Lumber Company grade sawing such products as moldings, windows, door units and material handling devices such as pallets.

In 1968, Lester Lumber manufactured solid and distributed panelized housing packages to builders including a floor, wall, roof systems, windows, doors, cabinets, and interior millwork. With less than sixty stockholders, the 1927 capitalization of $500,000 went to 10 million in 1969.

George Washington Lester II, born on April 4, 1939, was the last child of George Tilden and Lottie Floy Shelton Lester. He graduated from Martinsville High School in 1957. He graduated from North Carolina State University cum laude with a Bachelor's Degree in Industrial Engineering. He joined the company in 1959 and is now President and CEO of the Lester Group serving in that position since 1983.

His achievements include the 1989 opening of the 515,000 square foot 22 million-dollar Liberty Fair Mall on the site of the Liberty Heights Swimming Pool and Lester Airport along Liberty

Street. The Y-shaped 380 square foot mall sits on forty-two acre site along Commonwealth Boulevard.

He was instrumental in the development of Commonwealth Boulevard in including a Ford Dealership, Martinsville High School, and Memorial Hospital. Other businesses included Beaver Hills Development.

Today George W. Lester II is the CEO of the Lester Group (www.lestergroup.com), a multi-division company in the states of Virginia, West Virginia, and North Carolina. Lester Development started in 1974 has six shopping centers, freestanding restaurants, commercial and industrial buildings and seven Speedway Centers that are convenience stores and car washes. The company created Lester Square Shopping Center in Sophia, West Virginia, followed two years later by Hethwood Shopping Center in Blacksburg, Virginia. In 1987, Ridgewood Square Shopping Center and six years after that Leatherwood Shopping Center in Martinsville along with Liberty Fair Convenience Center were projects of the company. In 1997, the company built the Patrick Henry Shopping Center in Blacksburg. Three years earlier the Lester Group built Ryan's Steakhouse and Applebee's along Commonwealth Boulevard followed in 1998 by the Jameson Inn. Continuing to work in Spotsylvania County, Virginia's fastest growing area including Fredericksburg, Lester properties include the Mill Race Commons.

Another Fredericksburg division of the Lester Group is Jim Carpenter Company, a full service building materials supplier for professional builders, contractors, remodelers, and homeowners. The company provides a full line of interior and exterior products including lumber, plywood, windows, doors, and molding for engineered floor system designs.

Lester Properties manages and develops commercial, retail, residential and subdivision properties. The company has residential properties stretching from King Manor Apartments and homes on Fairy Street in Martinsville, the Lofts at the Lyric in Blacksburg and Huffman Street Apartments in Charlotte, North Carolina.

Fortress Wood Products provides customers with quality pressure treated lumber and board stock for commercial and residential building applications with facilities in the North Carolina communities of Greensboro, Henderson, Elizabeth City, and Enfield.

Another division of the Lester Group includes the Forestry Division. With over 18,000 acres of forestland in Rockingham County, North Carolina along with acreage in Franklin, Halifax, Henry and Pittsylvania counties in Virginia, this division carries on the original work of the Lester Lumber Company started in 1896. Hunting leases are available to groups to use the forestlands.

George once said, "I do believe in the community, and a company can only be as strong as the community it's in." Over the years he served on the United Way of Martinsville, Transportation Committee of the West Piedmont Planning District, Governor's Committee on Virginia Forest Resources, Board of the Martinsville Memorial Hospital, and the Martinsville Henry County Economic Development.

Professionally, George Washington Lester II served with the Virginia Forest Association, Independent Builders Supply Association, American Property Management Corporation, Homebuilders of Martinsville Henry County. Boards served on include the Patrick Henry National Bank and Shenandoah National Bank. An Elk, George is a member of the First Baptist Church of Martinsville.

In 1993, he started JobLink, a regional organization promoting the building of Interstate 73 from Roanoke to Piedmont North Carolina believing that a four-lane highway would bring much needed commerce to Henry County. The proposed road would bring travelers from as far north as Detroit, Michigan, to Myrtle Beach, South Carolina.

Ever looking forward to the future, the Lester Group purchased the former Tultex Corporation plant on Commonwealth Boulevard in 2001 for $750,000 in bankruptcy court. After investing over three million dollars to make the "building marketable" including grading a two tiered parking lot between Franklin and Liberty Streets, the Clock Tower at the Commonwealth Centre is today leasing at the 175,000 square foot complex. The building built by Rucker and Whittlen Plug Tobacco at the turn of the twentieth century. In the 1930s, Carolina Cotton bought the plant and in 1957, Sale Knitting, a spinoff of Pannill Knitting, purchased the building. Tultex as the last occupant of the building before the Lester Group bought the building.

G. W. Lester II serves on the Board of Directors of Carter Bank and Trust and is a Trustee of the New College Institute Foundation. In 2008, he served on the Board of the National Lumber and Building Material Dealers Association. His awards included the Heck Ford Award from the Martinsville Henry County Chamber of Commerce and the Clyde Hooker Award from Piedmont Arts Association.

He is the father of four children: Elizabeth, Ann, Sarah, and George Washington Lester IV. Elizabeth married Douglas K. Walsh in 1996. Sarah married James T. Jedelsky in 2002. George Washington Lester IV married Beth S. Jedelsky in 1999.

"It's not just about one person. It takes the support of the people around him. I moved to Martinsville in better times. But I'm convinced that the best times are still ahead."

George T. and Lottie Shelton Lester.

Chapter Thirteen
Ralph

Ralph Clayton Lester likes "to be first" in anything he does. Three times during his life he started businesses to make modular homes and three times he left those businesses prosperous and growing.

The son of Loury and Mamie Frances Lester, Ralph, spent his formative years growing up near Figsboro on the Lester Branch of Beaver Creek, where the Lesters first came to Henry County. He attended a one-room school, and then went to school on the Barrows Mill Road before spending his third year at Martinsville City Schools. With his older brother driving, Ralph went to Central Grammar School on Cleveland Avenue. He graduated from Martinsville High School in 1936.

During high school Ralph worked part time for his Uncle V. M. Draper on Depot Street. Nine months after graduation, he went to work with his father at a sawmill at seventy-five cents a day. Working for his uncle, George Tilden Lester, at Lester Lumber Company, Ralph made $500-600 a month on commission beginning in 1939.

Ralph served in the Virginia National Guard from 1936-39, but he realized the infantry was not for him. Like many other

Lesters he found his spot flying airplanes. After soloing in 1940, he joined the Army Air Force in July 1941. He got his "Wings" at Lockbourne Army Air Base in Columbus, Ohio. When World War Two erupted he went to New Guinea and later Australia. He trained to fly gliders, but spent most of the time flying DC-3 cargo planes ferrying supplies to McArthur's army in the Pacific.

    He tells of taking off in New Guinea ascending 12,000 feet and immediately descending after clearing the mountains and preparing to land. "We never had a chance to level off." Ralph Lester flew sixty-five combat missions rising to the rank of First Lieutenant. He sent most of pay home to his wife, the former Alice Saunders Lester, whom he married in 1942. Alice saved most of it leaving Ralph $16,000 in 1945 ($182,526.43 in 2007 value.) He built her a home on Forest Street using mules and drag pans to dig out the basement.

    In 1937, Ralph began building contract homes at age 18. He built four room frame houses on Chatham Road for $500-600, subcontracting made Ralph $100 in profit. In 1946, Ralph began Lester Brothers with his brothers Victor and Lawson. They sold building supplies and built houses on contract. Ralph learned the retail, wholesale, manufacturing, field construction, office, and sales giving his knowledge of financing. This business evolved into the Lesco Homes, which became part of National Enterprises of Lafayette, Indiana, formerly National Homes Corporation.

Victor Arlington Lester, born on April 26, 1915, to Loury and Mamie Draper Lester, graduated from Martinsville High School. He worked for Lester Lumber Company before World War Two. Before the war he was in the National Guard. Victor served in the Third Army in Europe fighting in the Battle of the Bulge. Victor continued working for Lester Brothers after National Homes bought it out and retired from that company in 1967. He married Louise Robertson. Victor Lester died on December 9, 1979.

Seeing the need for manufactured homes in 1955, Ralph started Continental Homes of Boones Mill that is today part of Wylan Inc. It filled a need for low cost homes and financing for buyers not qualified for government insured or government home financing. By making a small down payment and making monthly payments people could own their own home. Lester continued Continental Homes for another ten years as well. In 1968, Weil-McLain of Indiana purchased Continental in a one for one stock swap.

Four years later in September 1959, Ralph began Nationwide Homes with an office in Collinsville. Alice served as the first Secretary and Earle W. Greene as Vice-President. There were three homes "models" at the office completed a "various stages of construction." In 1959, bread cost twenty-two cents and gas was twenty-four cents a gallon. Ralph C. Lester began Nationwide with $100,000. He sold 200,000 shares at fifty cents a share. A year later he sold 100,000 shares for $1.50 a share raising $400,000. The shares were going for $9.50 a share on the local market. The company began making 200 homes its first year and by 1976 was making 1,500 with over $85 million in sales. The company was different as it financed construction of small housing plans for customers, "the working man." The basic idea was that customers got a "basic home." Depending on their "sweat equity," the ability to labor the homeowner wanted to put into it, the house came built as much as 90% complete. If you had a "piece of ground," there were seventeen different models from $5,000 to $10,000 with 95% "required financing." One employee Willie and his wife, Gracie W. Martin signed up to make 71 monthly payments of $46.45. Homes included a foundation, floor, walls, roof studs, ceiling, and electric wiring. The next year there were 90 homes within thirty miles of Martinsville. Between April 1960 and March 1961 there were 922 homes sold and 800 more in the next six months in Virginia, West Virginia, North and South Carolina, Maryland, Tennessee and Kentucky.

In August 1961, Nationwide went public with 3,300,000 shares underwritten by a national brokerage firm (300,000 shares at $6). Expansion began into twenty-seven branch offices with forty-two salaried employees and 200 commission salespeople selling fifty houses a week. Eight years later the company went from onsite building to factory building of the houses. That year, Nationwide built 5,000 homes in thirteen states. Eighteen months later a new plant was ready to manufacture modular homes. The 27,000 square foot plant and office was at 1100 Rives Road on 28 acres adjacent to the railroad. Seven years after that a 255,325 square foot facility opened for manufacturing and storage. Among the new structures manufactured were remote class rooms, modular units for schools. This author remembers classes in one of these Nationwide structures at Blue Ridge Elementary School in Ararat, Virginia.

While families always have dysfunctional areas, there is one thing that all Lesters have in common. Everyone likes Ralph. His employees share this feeling. One said of him that he was, "a great friend and a great man to work for." Ralph Lovell recalls his first day at Nationwide Homes in November 1971. It snowed and Lovell had no snow tires and began to walk to catch a bus to make his first day in the drafting department. As the 19 year old made his way up Rives Road, a Lincoln Continental pulled up alongside and gave Lovell a ride to the bus station. The next day at work Lovell was amazed to see the man who carried him to catch a bus to Nationwide Homes was the President of the company Ralph C. Lester.

Ralph Clayton Lester like many other members of his family believed strongly in giving back to the community and his profession. He served as President of the House Manufacturing Association in 1967. Two years later he received the Eugene E. Kurtz Award for his contributions to the development of manufactured housing. He worked tirelessly to bring the Salvation Army to Martinsville and once gave the Martinsville Henry County Chamber of Commerce $300 to purchase and distribute Economic textbooks to area schools. Ralph Lester served on Chamber committees along with the United Fund and Patrick Henry Community College. He served as a Deacon at Forest Hills Presbyterian Church. His civic organizations include the Kiwanis, Elk, Pythians, and the American Legion.

He and Alice had two children: Ralph C. Lester, Jr. and Elizabeth Lester Winn.

Ralph lost his father Loury Lawson Lester in 1975 at the age of 89. Loury worked for Lester Lumber Company until 1930 and then managed his own lumber operation for seven years. For the next twenty-three years he was a livestock farmer and cattle dealer, retiring in 1960. Today, an airport in Henry County bears his name. He had five daughters, Mrs. Ben A. Harris, Inez L. Montel, Mrs. Hyman Philips, Jr., Mrs. Ralph S. Lawson, and Mrs. B. M. Estes. Ralph's brothers were Lawson and Victor. Loury Lawson Lester left fourteen grandchildren and nine great-grandchildren.

Nationwide started an "Owner Completion Program" that gave "instant equity" to the customers. In 1982, the company projects into condominiums and apartment projects. In 1995, Nationwide built 20,000 modular. The company acquired Arabi Homes in Georgia.

Nationwide Homes continued to expand with manufacturing facilities on thirteen acres in Siler City, North Carolina, and twenty-one acres in Arabi, Georgia, along with 500 employees in Martinsville. The company has homes in sixteen states from Pennsylvania to Florida, Delaware to Indiana and south to Louisiana.

Ralph C. Lester retired in 1979. Family and local history became a passion for him. This book would not exist without the hours of interviews and his willingness to share his incredible breadth of knowledge about this history. He received the James R. Price Award in 1987 as "Man of the Year" in Automation in

Housing and Manufactured Home Dealers. They described Ralph as the "Father of the modern modular housing industry."

Loury Lester and his son Ralph Lester.

First Family Reunion
Ralph C. Lester and George Oakley, other not identified.

Chapter Fourteen

Lester Images

Above George Oakley and George Lester, grandson and son of George T. "Capt'n Till" Lester at the Koehler "Castle," shown below.

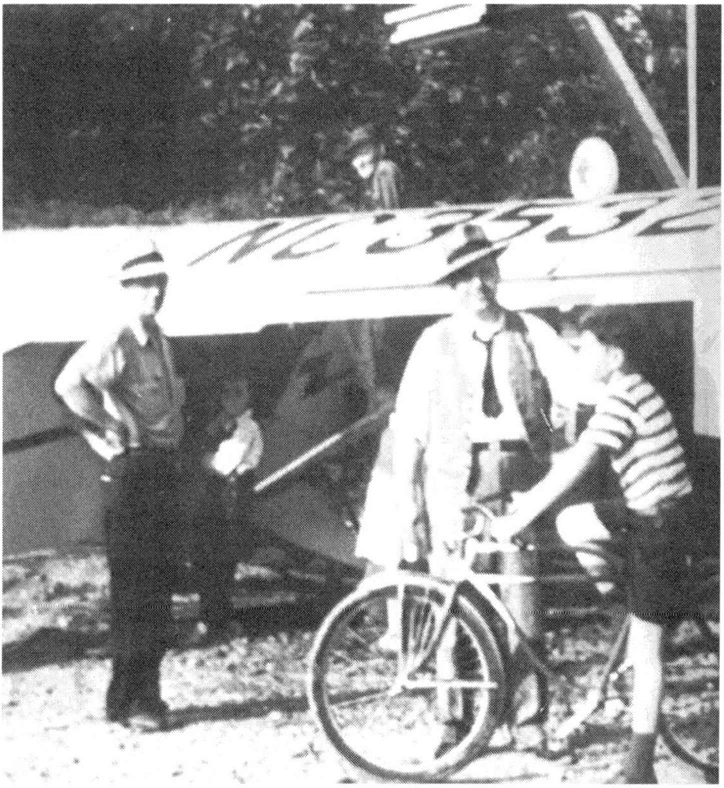

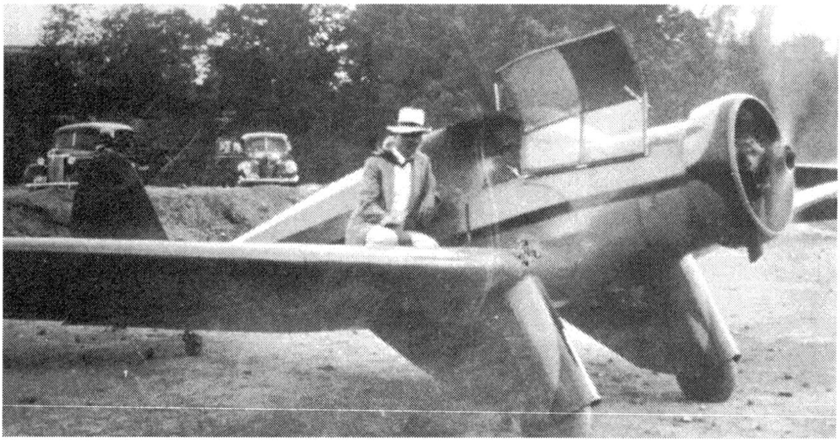

Liberty Street Airport with swimming pool in background above and below along Liberty Street.

Above Liberty Street Airport and Barrow Mills below.

Flint Hill Plantation near Barrow's Mill site.

162

George Tilden "Capt'n Till" Lester.

George T. and Lottie Shelton Lester at the Wedding Cake House.

Gravesite of George Washington Lester with Ralph and George Lester visiting their mutual ancestor in 2009.

165

Final resting place of Henry Clay Lester in Oakdale Cemetery.

Graves of William Lester and others near Figsboro.

Grave of George T. "Capt'n Till" Lester.

Civil War Prison Camp at Point Lookout, Maryland, where like the soldiers below, George W. Lester was imprisoned.

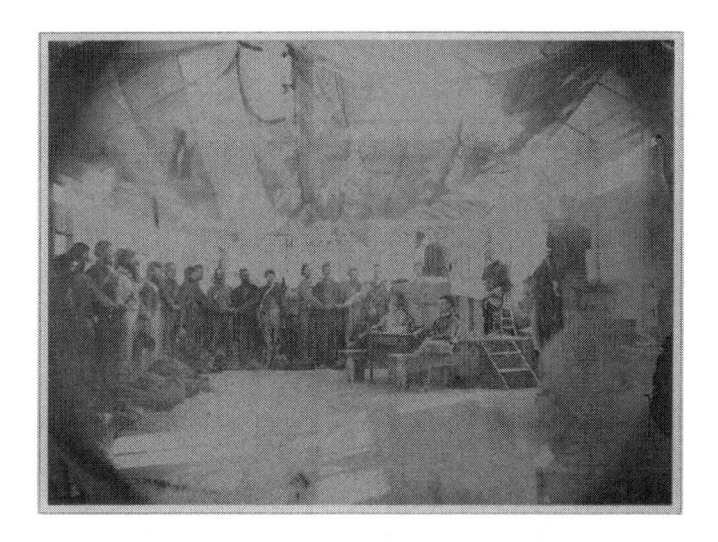

The Wedding Cake House of the Lesters on Starling Avenue in Martinsville, Virginia, was listed in the book *Weird Virginia.*

Application of Soldier, Sailor or Marine for a Pension,
Disabled by Reason of Disease or Other Infirmities.

I, Geo. W. Lester, a native of the State of Virginia, and now a citizen of Virginia, resident at Wasp in the County (or city) of Carroll in said State of Virginia, and who was a soldier from the State of Va, in the war between the United States and the Confederate States, do hereby apply for aid under an act of the General Assembly, approved March 7, 1900, entitled "An act to give aid to soldiers, sailors, and marines disabled in the war between the States, and to every such soldier, sailor, or marine who by disease or other infirmities of age, is disabled from earning or is without the means of procuring a support, and to the widows of Virginia soldiers, sailors, or marines who lost their lives in said war in the military or naval service, or whose husbands have died since the war." And I do solemnly swear that I was a member of Company A 24th Virginia Regiment and that I am now disabled by reason of disease and infirmities of age, loss of eyesight and that by reason of such disability I am now entitled to receive, under said Act, the sum of fifteen dollars, annually. I further swear that I do not hold any National, State, or County office which pays me in salary or fees over three hundred dollars per annum; nor have I an income from any other source which amounts to three hundred dollars; nor do I own in my own right, nor does my wife own, property of the assessed value of more than one thousand dollars; nor do I receive aid or a pension from any other State or from the United States; and that I am not an inmate of any soldier's home.

I do further swear that the following answers are true:

1st. What is the applicant's age? Ans. 63 yrs
2d. What is the precise nature of the disability of the applicant? loss of eye sight
Ans. disease of kidneys, and other disease and infirmities of age
3d. Is it total? Ans. No
(a) Is it partial? and, if so, to what extent does it disable him from manual labor? Ans. yes: incapacitates me from earning a living from manual labor

Given under my hand this 29th day of May, 1900.

Witness
M. P. Ogle

Geo. W. Lester
mark

I, J. M. Brown, a Commissioner in Chancery for the Circuit Court of Carroll County, do certify that Geo. W. Lester, whose name is signed to the foregoing application, personally appeared before me in my county aforesaid, and having the aforesaid application read to him and fully explained, as well as the statements and answers therein made, he, the said Geo. Lester, made oath before me that the said statements and answers are true.

Given under my hand, this 29th day of May, 1900.

J. M. Brown, Com. in Chancery

In the Circuit Court of the County of Carroll on the 16th day of July, 1900. The application of Geo. W. Lester for a Pension, with the certificate of the Chairman of the Confederate Pension Board of the County (or City) of ...., that it has been approved by said Board thereon endorsed, was presented to the Court; and the Clerk of this Court is directed to certify a copy of this order to the Auditor of Public Accounts.

I, H. Luther Land, Clerk of the County Court of the county (or city) of Carroll, do certify that the foregoing is a true copy from the Records of said Court.

Civil War Pension Application of George Washington Lester.

FRIDAY, DEC. 7, 1917. $1.00 a Year. Single Copy 5 Cents

ER AND ELECTRIC POWER Henry County 20,000

PATRICK COUNTY MAN MEETS DEATH IN ROANOKE

Mr. Walter H. Clark, merchant and with his wife and two children had spent Thanksgiving at the home of Mrs. Clark's uncle Mr. Asa Howard, in Roanoke, was run down and instantly killed by a street car about half past six o'clock on the morning of the 30th as he was on his way to the Norfolk & Western station. As Mrs. Clark and the children had remained for a longer visit he was alone. The car was an empty on its way to the business section, so the only witness of the tragedy was the motorman, who claims he didn't see the man in the darkness. Mr. Clark was a second cousin of Mr. T. L. Clark, deputy U. S. Marshal of Martinsville. A Bulletin reporter interviewed Mr. Clark, but could only gather the foregoing brief facts, as the friends and relatives are without details because there were no witnesses.

The deceased was superintendent of the Methodist Sunday School in Stuart, and grand lecturer of the Masonic order for this district, and has a wide circle of friends who are shocked at the news of his tragic death.

She Is Not Dead But Sleepeth

Entire Community Shocked Friday Morning By The Sad News.

MRS. LESTER HAD JUST RETURNED FROM JOHNS-HOPKINS HOSPITAL

The many friends of Mrs. G. T. Lester are saddened by her death which took place about seven o'clock on the night of Thanksgiving day at her home in Martinsville. Mrs. Lester had returned only the day before from Johns Hopkins hospital, where she had undergone an operation about three weeks before. She felt that she was getting along well enough so she could go home and telegraphed her husband to come and get her. It was a happy home, on Thanksgiving day with wife and mother home again, an occasion long to be remembered. She was feeling real well, for the short time that had elapsed since the operation, but early in the evening she felt fatigued and retired, death coming on silent wings, swiftly, but with the ease of a whisper.

Mrs. Lester was Miss Parker Turner of Roanoke, daughter of Mr. and Mrs. C. M. Turner of that city, and she married Mr. Lester about thirteen years ago. She was a woman of beautiful nature, a devoted wife and mother, and a steadfast and consistant friend, one deeply mourned by those of whom she was dearly beloved.

She is survived by her husband and five children, the two younger children being twins. She also survived by her father; two brothers, M. W. Turner of Roanoke, and Henry Turner of Tennessee, and sister Mrs. Della Wicklline of Washington, D. C.

Services were held on November 30, under the form of the Primitive Baptist denomination, Elder A. L. Moore officiating, and the beloved remains laid to rest in Oakwood cemetery.

Paul bearers were Messrs G. A. Brown, J. L. Stultz, Sr, W. D. Belton, J. A. Brown, T. C Matthews, W J. Lester, and Dr. R. R. Lee.

Flower bearers were Messrs E. J. Davis, J. D. Stultz, J. B. Coleman, W. J. Lester, and Mr. Richardson.

Appropriate hymns were sung by Mrs. E. B. Semple, Mrs. A. N. Hodges, and Messrs W. B. Baron...

SHOP EARLY
ONLY
15
More Shopping Days Until
XMAS

Parker Lester death announcement.

Entrance to the Lester Family Cemetery near Dyer's Store.

George Lester as a young man and as head of the Lester Group.

GEORGE W. LESTER, II

Rucker-Witten Tobacco Company under construction in 1899 and below in 2009 as part of the Lester Group's Commonwealth Center after a stint as Tultex.

Lester Lumber Company before and after fire destroyed it.

Lester Lumber Company

Lester Lumber Co., Inc., Martinsville, Va.

177

Site Liberty Fair Mall today above, notice swimming pool on far left, and Lester Lumber Company, below.

Views of Liberty Heights Swimming Pool.

179

M-2 INTERIOR OF LIBERTY HEIGHTS SWIMMING POOL, MARTINSVILLE, VA.

181

182

183

Conclusion
The Lesters and Henry County

In 1990, Julia Lester Oakley was still walking and talking about her family history. Although legally blind and a diabetic, she took her ski pole and walked around the block repeatedly near her house. She recorded tapes about her family's history that this author used transcriptions.

The oldest child of George Tilden Lester, Sr. said her father taught her when she stopped learning, she might as well be dead. She attended Central Grammar School in Martinsville and Martha Washington College before marrying George Dillard "Doc" Oakley. They had five children Julia, Sally, George, John, and Robert. "Life is wonderful for people who can see the beauty of it. I don't know if I deserve all the good I get, but I am sure thankful for it." Julia never left Henry County for very long. "I've always been too happy within myself and my family. My father never got away either; I guess got it from him." George died in 1984, but Julia continued for another twenty years dying on January 29, 2004.

Ralph C. Lester said to me in the course of writing this book, "I have lived in the most interesting period of history." His cousin, George Washington Lester II chimed in saying, "We have been blessed. We have lived in the best country in the best time and the best place in the world." Such is the history of the Lester Family of Henry County Virginia and their upward toil from the farm to the heights of business.

.

Appendix
Senate Resolution No. 383
Patents of George Tilden Lester
Family Tree of the Lester Family

SENATE JOINT RESOLUTION NO. 383
Offered January 24, 1997
Commending The Lester Group.

Consent to introduce

WHEREAS, in 1896, George T. (Cap'n Til) Lester founded the Lester Lumber Company, a small sawmill and planing mill; and

WHEREAS, a century later, The Lester Group, as it is now called, celebrated 100 years of service to the citizens of Martinsville and Henry County; and

WHEREAS, The Lester Group has grown steadily over the years, adding products and services, expanding into such areas as wood products, building supplies, forest management, property management, and development; and

WHEREAS, now one of the most successful businesses in the area, The Lester Group, still family held, contributes in numerous ways to the economy of Martinsville and Henry County; and

WHEREAS, indicative of its long-term commitment to the growth and development of Martinsville and Henry County, The Lester Group has contributed land for public buildings and roadways, provided leadership in area-wide economic development efforts, and donated to a wide range of worthy causes; and

WHEREAS, The Lester Group has donated land for the Memorial Hospital of Martinsville and Henry County, has played an instrumental role in bringing new businesses and employment opportunities to the area, and has promoted a number of important economic development initiatives over the years; and

WHEREAS, for a century, The Lester Group has grown and prospered along with Martinsville and Henry County, has contributed in numerous ways to the economic well-being of the area, and has proven itself many times over as a corporate good citizen; now, therefore, be it

RESOLVED by the Senate, the House of Delegates concurring, That the General Assembly commend The Lester Group on the occasion of its centennial celebration; and, be it

RESOLVED FURTHER, That the Clerk of the Senate prepare a copy of this resolution for presentation to George W. Lester II, President and Chief Executive Officer of The Lester Group, as an expression of the General Assembly's appreciation for the company's manifold contributions to Martinsville, Henry County, and the Commonwealth.

No. 683,951. Patented Oct. 8, 1901.
G. T. LESTER.
PLUG TOBACCO MACHINE.
(Application filed May 21, 1901.)

(No Model.) 9 Sheets—Sheet 1.

Fig. 1.

Witnesses
Inventor
George T. Lester
By H. R. Wilson & Co.
Attorneys

No. 683,951.
G. T. LESTER.
PLUG TOBACCO MACHINE.
(Application filed May 21, 1901.)
Patented Oct. 8, 1901.

(No Model.)

9 Sheets—Sheet 2.

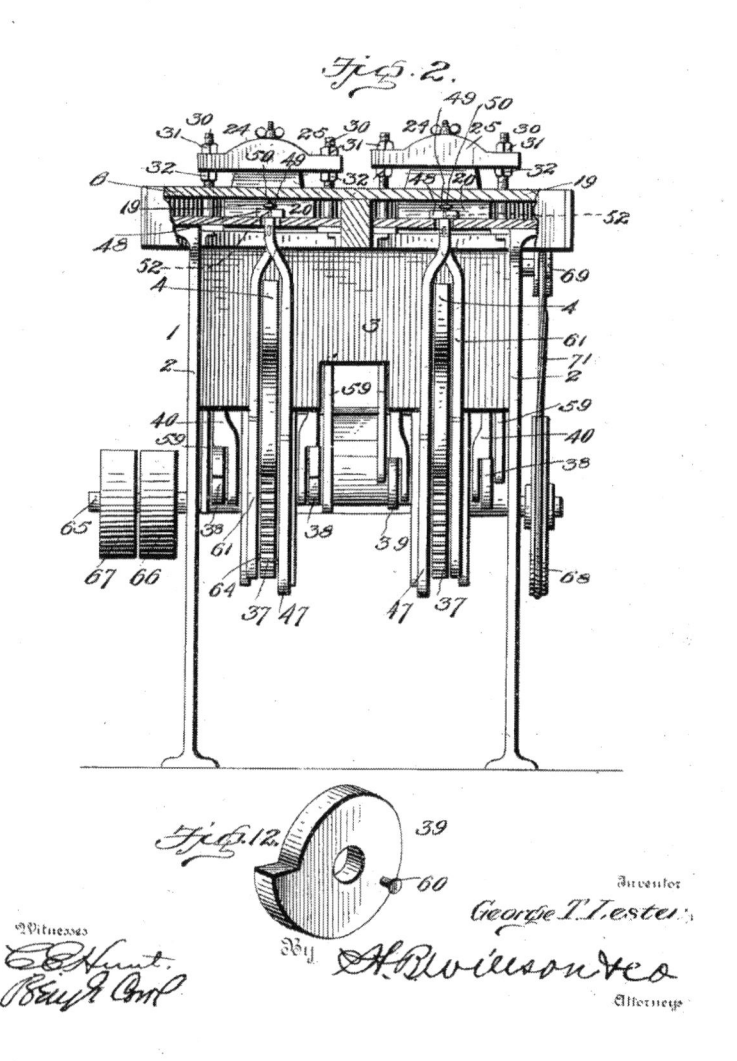

No. 683,951. Patented Oct. 8, 1901.
G. T. LESTER.
PLUG TOBACCO MACHINE.
(Application filed May 21, 1901.)
(No Model.) 9 Sheets—Sheet 3.

No. 683,951. Patented Oct. 8, 1901.
G. T. LESTER.
PLUG TOBACCO MACHINE.
(Application filed May 21, 1901.)

(No Model.) 9 Sheets—Sheet 4.

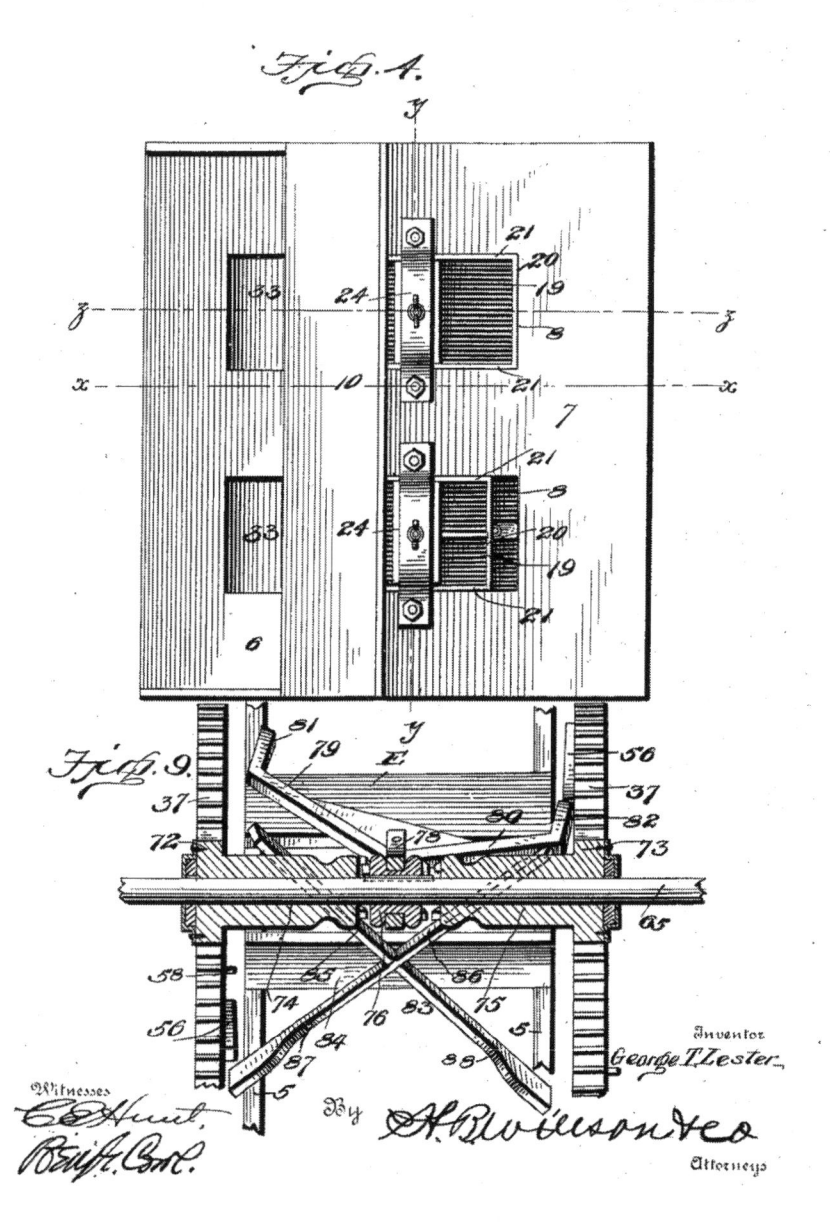

No. 683,951. Patented Oct. 8, 1901.
G. T. LESTER.
PLUG TOBACCO MACHINE.
(Application filed May 21, 1901.)

(No Model.) 9 Sheets—Sheet 5.

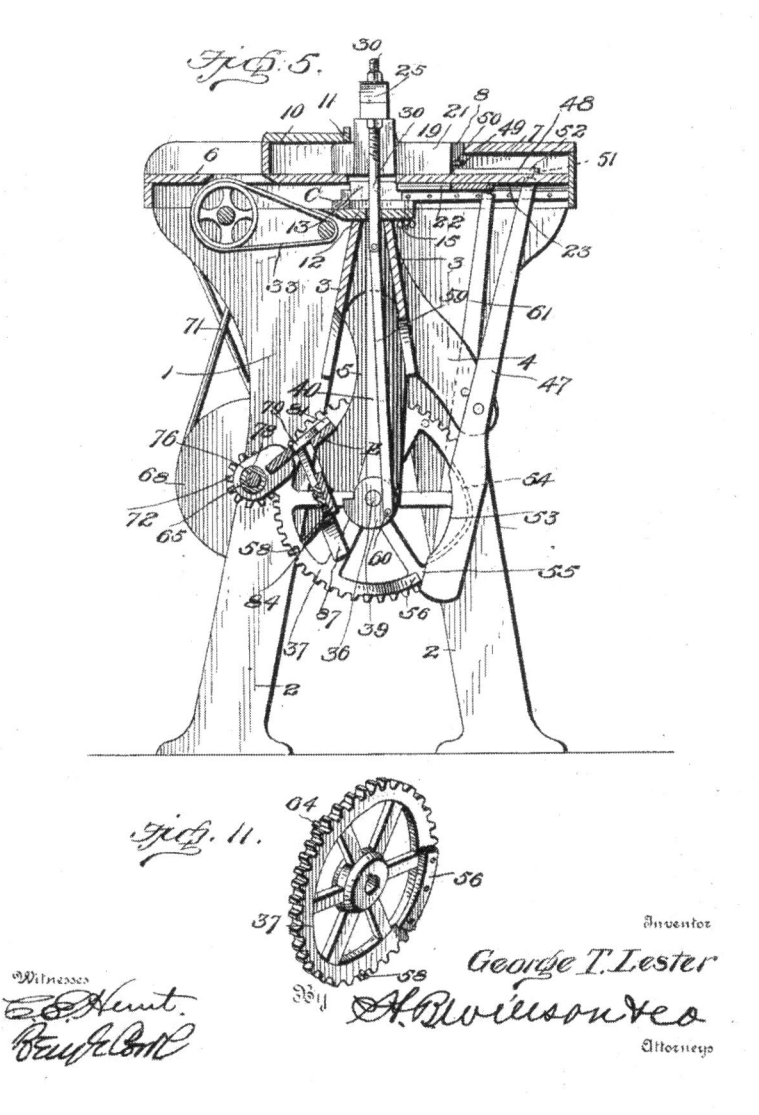

Inventor
George T. Lester
By H. B. Willson & Co.
Attorneys

Witnesses

No. 683,951. Patented Oct. 8, 1901.
G. T. LESTER.
PLUG TOBACCO MACHINE.
(Application filed May 21, 1901.)

(No Model.) 9 Sheets—Sheet 6.

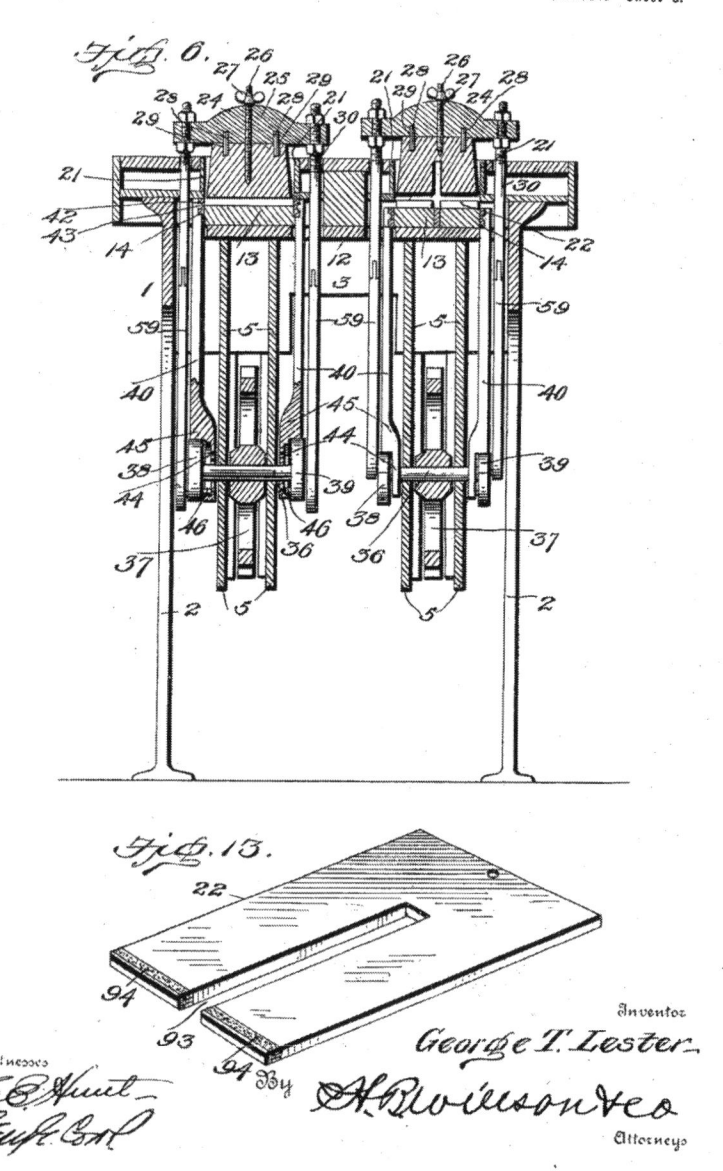

Fig. 6.

Fig. 13.

Witnesses
Inventor
George T. Lester
By H. B. Wilson & Co.
Attorneys

No. 683,951. **Patented Oct. 8, 1901.**
G. T. LESTER.
PLUG TOBACCO MACHINE.
(Application filed May 21, 1901.)

(No Model.) 9 Sheets—Sheet 7.

Fig. 7.

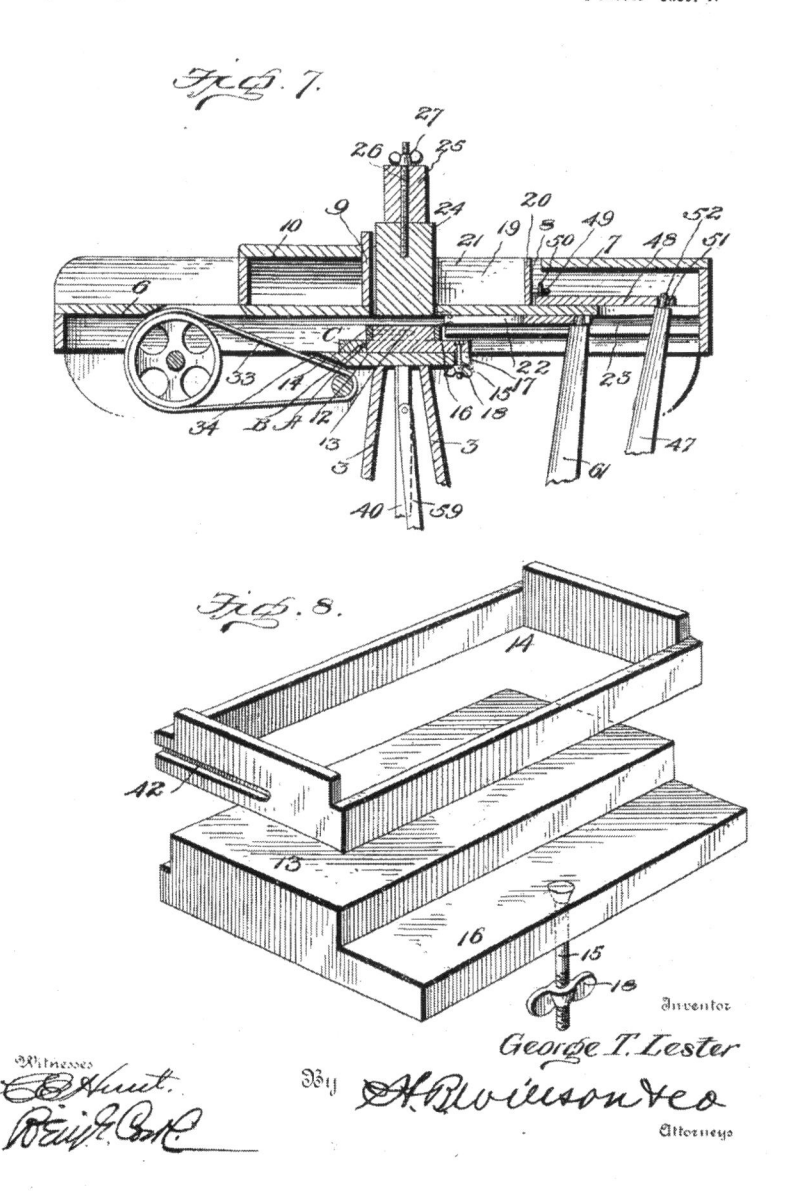

Fig. 8.

Witnesses

Inventor
George T. Lester
By H. B. Willson & Co
Attorneys

No. 683,951. Patented Oct. 8, 1901.
G. T. LESTER.
PLUG TOBACCO MACHINE.
(Application filed May 21, 1901.)

(No Model.) 9 Sheets—Sheet 8.

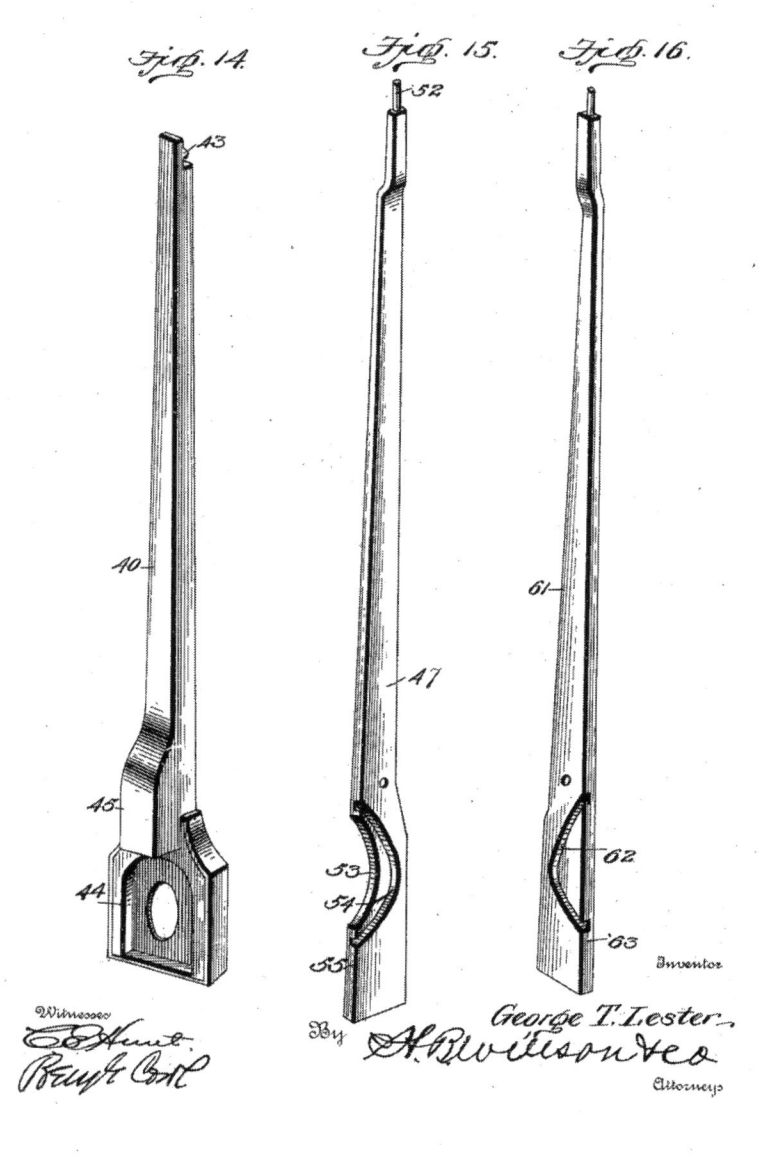

Fig. 14. Fig. 15. Fig. 16.

Witnesses Inventor
George T. Lester,
By H. B. Willson & Co.
Attorneys

No. 683,951. Patented Oct. 8, 1901.

G. T. LESTER.

PLUG TOBACCO MACHINE.

(Application filed May 21, 1901.)

(No Model.) 9 Sheets—Sheet 9.

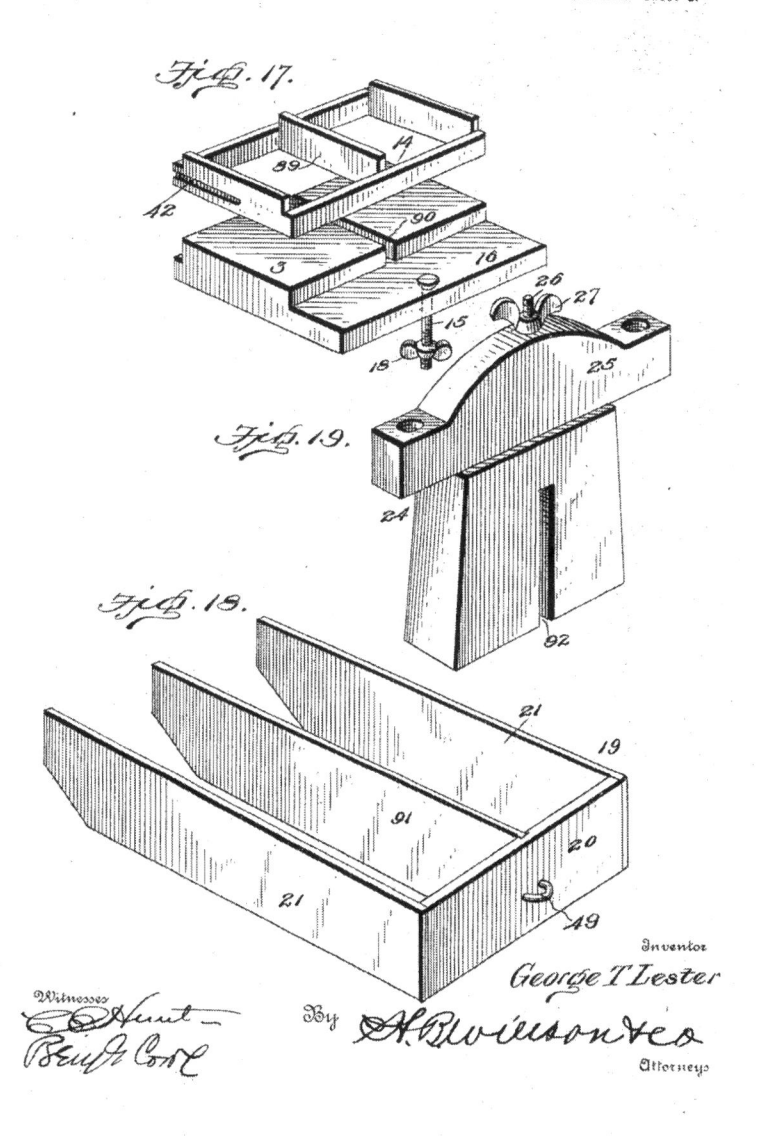

Fig. 17.

Fig. 19.

Fig. 18.

Inventor

George T Lester

Witnesses

C. D. Hunt

Benj. G. Cowl

By H. B. Willson & Co

Attorneys

UNITED STATES PATENT OFFICE.

GEORGE T. LESTER, OF DYER STORE, VIRGINIA.

PLUG-TOBACCO MACHINE.

SPECIFICATION forming part of Letters Patent No. 683,951, dated October 8, 1901.

Application filed May 21, 1901. Serial No. 61,262. (No model.)

To all whom it may concern:

Be it known that I, GEORGE T. LESTER, a citizen of the United States, residing at Dyer Store, in the county of Henry and State of Virginia, have invented certain new and useful Improvements in Plug-Tobacco Machines; and I do declare the following to be a full, clear, and exact description of the invention, such as will enable others skilled in the art to which it appertains to make and use the same.

The invention relates to a plug-tobacco machine designed more particularly for giving the initial pressure to the filler or body of the plug before the binder or wrapper is put on and for discharging said plugs continuously and consecutively from the machine without lessening, breaking, or destroying in any way the integrity of the plug, which after being provided with a wrapper and dried is subjected to a heavy final pressure in another machine.

The object of the invention is to provide a machine of this character which shall be simple of construction, durable in use, comparatively inexpensive of production, efficient in action, and which may be easily and quickly changed to press plugs into different forms or sizes.

With these and other objects in view, the invention consists of certain novel features of construction, combination, and arrangement of parts, which will be hereinafter more fully described, and particularly pointed out in the appended claims.

In the accompanying drawings, Figure 1 is a rear perspective view of the complete machine. Fig. 2 is a front elevation of the same with parts shown in section. Fig. 3 is a rear view of the machine. Fig. 4 is a top plan view. Fig. 5 is a longitudinal vertical sectional view on line $x\,x$, Fig. 4. Fig. 6 is a transverse sectional view on line $y\,y$, Fig. 4, showing the plunger at one side of the machine in its elevated position and the plunger at the other side of the machine in its depressed position. Fig. 7 is a vertical sectional view on line $z\,z$, Fig. 4. Fig. 8 is a perspective view of one style of mold-box, the parts being shown separate. Fig. 9 is a vertical longitudinal sectional view through the parts mounted on the main drive-shaft. Fig. 10 is a front view of the clutch-shipper and its actuating-lever. Fig. 11 is a perspective view of one of the master-gears. Fig. 12 is a similar view of one of the cams. Fig. 13 is a similar view of one of the ejectors. Fig. 14 is a perspective view of one of the mold-box-operating bars. Fig. 15 is a similar view of one of the feeder-actuating levers. Fig. 16 is a similar view of one of the ejector-actuating levers. Fig. 17 is a perspective view of a mold-box for forming two plugs at one operation of the plunger, the parts of the mold-box being shown separated. Fig. 18 is a similar view of one of the feeders to coöperate with said mold-box, and Fig. 19 is a similar view of one of the coacting plungers.

In the drawings, 1 denotes the main frame of the machine, consisting of vertical standards or side pieces 2, connected at their upper ends by cross-pieces 3, one of which has downwardly and forwardly projecting arms 4. Two sets of hanger-arms 5 project downwardly from between the cross-pieces 3 and support the operating-shafts hereinafter referred to.

6 denotes the table, secured to the upper ends of the vertical side pieces or standards. Supported over the front portion and extending the full width thereof is a shelf 7, having feed-openings 8 and a vertical partition 9, Fig. 7, to the rear of which is arranged an inclosing hood 10. The partition 9 is formed with vertical slots 11, Fig. 5, for the purpose of permitting of the reciprocation of the feeders under the plungers, as hereinafter explained.

12 denotes a platform fixed to or cast integral with the upper edges of the cross-pieces 3 and is designed to support the mold-boxes. Each mold-box consists of a stationary bottom 13, Figs. 7 and 8, and a surrounding vertically-movable frame 14. Each mold-box is secured to the platform 12 by a bolt 15, which extends through a hole in the ledge 16 of the bottom 13 and through a slot 17 in the edge of the platform and is provided with a tightening-nut 18. The rear edge of the stationary bottom has points or prongs A, which project into sockets B, formed in a cleat C, secured to the platform 12. This construction permits of the quick removal of the mold for

purposes of repair or when it is desired to replace it with one of a different shape, size, or design.

19 denotes feeders, each of which has a reciprocatory movement upon the table 6 and may be charged with tobacco through the feed-openings 8. Each of these feeders consists of an end piece 20 and side pieces 21, the rear ends of which extend through the slots 10 of the partition 9, and thus guide the feeders in their sliding movement as the feeder, with its charge of tobacco, moves over the mold-box.

24 denotes plungers designed to coöperate with the mold-boxes. The plungers are connected to cross-heads 25 by bolt 26 and nut 27 and are prevented from turning with respect to said heads by studs 28, Fig. 6, which project over the plunger into sockets 29, formed in the under side of the cross-heads. Each cross-head has connected to its ends rods 30, which extend through the shelf and table of the machine and operate in a manner hereinafter described. The connection of the rods with the cross-heads is such as to permit of the vertical adjustment of said cross-heads on said rods to limit the vertical movement of the plungers to which the cross-heads are attached, and thereby vary the degree of pressure upon the tobacco acted upon. Tightening-nuts 31 and jam-nuts 32, Fig. 2, are shown in the present instance as the means for effecting this adjustment.

22 denotes ejectors mounted to slide on suitably-mounted tracks 23. These ejectors move beneath the table 6 and are designed to eject the compressed plugs from the mold-boxes.

In operation the tobacco is weighed and placed into one of the feeders, which moves it onto the mold-box bottom under the elevated plunger. The movable frame of the mold-box is now elevated, and about the same time the plunger begins to descend and continues its downward movement between the sides and end of the feeder and the partition 9 into the mold-box. A slight pause or halt in the movement of the plunger now takes place, so as to temporarily hold the plug under compression, and thereby cause it to retain its shape when pressure has been removed. As soon as the plunger enters the mold-box the feeder is retracted and is in position to be refilled with a fresh charge of tobacco, which is done while the plunger is holding the plug under compression. After the plug has been held under compression a predetermined period of time the plunger and movable frame of the mold-box are simultaneously moved in opposite directions, the former upwardly and the latter downwardly, until its upper edge is flush with the bottom of the mold-box, and at this instant the ejector is shot rearwardly to throw the plug off the mold-box bottom and is instantly retracted. The plunger having been elevated and the frame of the mold-box lowered, the feeder, with its fresh charge of tobacco, now moves over the mold-box and under the plunger and the operation just described repeated to form another plug. After having been discharged from the mold-box bottom by the ejector the compressed plug falls upon an endless apron or conveyer 33, the upper run of which is on an incline and moves into contact with the end wall 34 and the opening at each side of the machine near the rear end of the table, so that the plug is thrown or discharged upon said table and may be gathered therefrom for the purpose of putting on a binder or wrapper.

I shall now proceed to describe the mechanism for operating the movable frame of the mold-box, and as this mechanism is duplicated on each side of the machine a description of one will answer for that of the other.

Journaled in the lower ends of the arms 5 (see Fig. 6) is a shaft 36, having fixed to it a toothed master-wheel 37 and cams 38 and 39. 40 denotes the bars for elevating and lowering the movable frame of the mold-box. The ends of the movable frame of the mold-box are provided with transverse grooves 42, Fig. 8, which are engaged by laterally-projecting tongues 43, formed at the upper ends of the bar 40. These grooves are open at the rear ends to permit of the withdrawal in a forward direction of the mold-box from engagement with the tongues of said bars when it is desired to substitute a mold-box of a different form or size. It will of course be understood that the nut 18 is loosened to permit the bottom of the mold-box to be moved forwardly with the movable frame thereof. The lower ends of the bars 40 are provided with yokes 44 and also with an offset 45. The bars of the mold-box are elevated in unison by the cams 39 engaging the offsets 45, and while their weight would in most cases cause them, with their connected mold-box frame, to descend I prefer to provide a positive means for effecting this, and to that end employ pins 46, projecting laterally from the inner faces of the cams and engaging the yokes 44. It will thus be seen that the rotary movement of the operating-shaft 36 is converted into a reciprocatory movement and this movement transmitted to the movable frame of the mold-box for reciprocating it.

The feeders hereinbefore referred to are operated in the following manner, and as the mechanism for operating each feeder is the same a description of one will answer for that of the other. Pivoted to one side of the arm 4 is a lever 47, (see Figs. 2 and 5,) the upper end of which is connected by a link 48 to the feeder, preferably by providing the forward end of the feeder with a staple 49, which is engaged by a pin 50, projecting upwardly from the rear end of said link with an eye 51, which is engaged by a pin 52, projecting upwardly from the end of the lever 47. The master-wheel is mounted directly under the longitudinal center of the feeder, and in order to connect the upper end of the lever to the longitudinal center portion of the feeder the said end is offset, as shown in Figs. 2 and 15. The rear edge of the lever 47 below its pivotal point is provided with a curved recess 53, and the outer side of said lever is provided with a cam-groove 54. The rear edge of said lever below the recess 53 is straight, as shown at 55. The master-wheel 37, Fig. 11, is provided on its inner face, near its periphery, with a segmental concentric block 56 and with a short pin 58, projecting laterally and arranged at a distance from said block. Assuming the feeder to have just been charged with tobacco, the rotation of the master-wheel will first bring the block 56 against the straight edge 55 of the lever and force the lower end of said lever forwardly and the upper end of said lever rearwardly, with its attached feeder, over the mold-box and under the plunger. The instant the block rises from engagement with the straight portion 55 of the lever its curved edge engages the curved recess 53 and temporarily holds the lever in its shifted position, with the feeder inclosing the plunger during the movement of the plunger downwardly into the mold-box, and the movable frame of the mold-box reaches the limit of its upward stroke before the plunger begins to descend into the mold-box, and by the shape of the cam the mold-box frame remains in its elevated position until the plunger has reached the limit of its downstroke, at about which instant the pin 58 of the master-wheel engages the cam-groove 54 of the lever 47, swings the lower end of said lever rearwardly and the upper end forwardly, and thus withdraws the feeder from the mold-box in a position to be recharged with tobacco to supply the mold-box.

I will now proceed to describe the mechanism for operating the plungers, and as this mechanism is duplicated on each side of the machine a description of one mechanism will answer for that of the other. 59, Figs. 3 and 5, denotes pitmen connected at their upper ends to the bars 30 of the cross-head and at their lower ends to crank-pins 60, projecting from the sides of the cams 39. As the cams rotate, as previously described, said pitmen will be reciprocated, thus lowering and raising the cross-head, with its attached plunger, into and out of the mold-box.

I will now proceed to describe the mechanism for operating the ejectors, and as each mechanism for each ejector is the same a description of one will answer for that of the other. 61, Figs. 16 and 5, denotes a lever pivoted to the outer face of the arm 4 and having a pin-slot connection at its upper end with the forward end of the ejector and provided at its lower end below its pivotal point with the arm 4, with a cam-groove 62, and having a straight rearward edge 63. After the tobacco has been depressed by the plunger and at the instant the mold-box frame descends and its upper edges become flush with the bottom of said box a pin 64, Fig. 11, projecting laterally from the face of the master-wheel, strikes the straight edge 63 of the lever 61 and suddenly throws the lower end of said lever forwardly and the upper end rearwardly with its ejector, which ejector knocks the compressed plug off the bottom of mold-box onto the endless conveyer in a manner previously described. The pin 64 next rides into the cam-groove 62 and retracts or withdraws the ejector from over the mold-box bottom.

The machine thus described is what might be properly termed a "duplex" machine, the tobacco being fed to the mold-boxes alternately and the plugs discharged therefrom in a like manner. While the plug is being compressed in the mold-box at one side of the machine, the mold-box at the other side of the machine is in condition to receive a charge of tobacco. To operate these two different sets of tobacco-compressing devices in alternation, I provide a novel form of mechanism, which I will now proceed to describe.

65 denotes the main drive-shaft, provided with loose and fixed pulleys 66 and 67, respectively, at one end and with a pulley 68 at the opposite end. The pulley 68 is connected to pulleys 69 and 70, fixed to the ends of the rollers of the endless conveyer 33 by a cross-belt 71 to drive said conveyer. 72 and 73 denote drive-pinions loosely mounted on said shaft 65 and meshing with the master-wheel 37. Clutch members 74 and 75 are fixed to these drive-pinions, preferably cast integral therewith, and are also loose upon said shaft. 76 denotes a clutch-head keyed to said shaft to rotate therewith and slide longitudinally thereon to alternately engage and lock the clutch members to said shaft to rotate in unison therewith. The clutch-shipper consists of a head-block 78, which fits an annular groove in the clutch-head and permits of the free rotation of said clutch-head. Pivoted to the head-block, to swing or rock transversely of said head-block, are two rigidly-connected forked arms 79 and 80, the extremities 81 and 82 of which project an angle to the length of the arms and rest or are supported upon a shelf E and are adapted to be alternately brought within the path of movement of the segmental blocks 56 of the master-wheels.

83 is a shipper-operating lever, preferably in the form of the letter X, pivoted to a cross-piece 84, secured to the lower ends of the arms 5, and having its arms 85 and 86 projecting upwardly and adapted to coact with the forked arms 79 and 80 and having its arms 87 and 88 projecting downwardly and adapted to be alternately engaged by the segmental blocks of the master-wheels.

Referring to Fig. 9 and assuming that the drive-shaft is in operation and the plungers at their lowest point in their respective boxes and the arm 82 of the shipper located in the path of movement of the block of the master-wheel with which it engages, the instant the end of the block strikes the end 82 of the arm 80 said arm is rocked to shift the shipper-head to disengage the clutch-head from the clutch member 75, thus instantly bringing that side of the machine operated by the master-wheel just described to a full stop, thus leaving the tobacco under pressure of the plunger, which is allowed to remain within the mold-box a predetermined period, as hereinbefore described. At the instant the clutch-head is disengaged from the clutch member 75 it is engaged with the clutch member 74, which causes said member 74 and its connected drive-pinion to rotate with the drive-shaft, and this rotary movement of the drive-shaft is transmitted to the other master-wheel, which in rotating will bring its segmental block into engagement with the arm 87 of the X-lever, thus rocking said lever and causing its arm 86 to engage the arm 80 and remove it from engagement with and out of the path of movement of the segmental block of the master-wheel, which has been brought to a period of rest. This movement of the arm 82 out of the path of movement of the segmental block is permitted by reason of the fact that the clutch-head 76, even while locked to the clutch member 74, has a slight lateral movement on the shaft 65 toward said clutch member, and thereby permits the arm 82 to free itself from its coacting segmental block when said arm is knocked upwardly by the arm 86 of the X-lever. In throwing the arm 80 to one side of the path of movement of the block with which it coacts the other arm 79 is thrown into the path of movement with the block with which it coacts. Now upon a further rotation of the master-wheel its block will be brought into engagement with the end 81 of the arm 79 and the wheel will be automatically stopped and the clutch-head shifted to cause the rotation of the opposite master-wheel. It will thus be seen that the compressing devices are worked alternately and that each plug within the mold-box is allowed to remain therein under compression a predetermined period of time, so as to prevent it from swelling or becoming otherwise distorted.

From the foregoing description, taken in connection with the accompanying drawings, the construction, mode of operation, and advantages of my invention will be readily understood without requiring a more extended explanation.

Various changes in the form, proportion, and details of construction may be made within the scope of the invention without departing from the spirit or sacrificing any of the advantages thereof. For instance, if it be desired to press two plugs instead of one at each stroke of the plunger I will change the mold-box, the feeder, and the plunger, as shown in Figs. 17, 18, and 19, respectively, wherein the only change is the provision in the movable frame of the mold-box of a partition 89 and in the bottom of the mold-box of a receiving-groove 90, in the feeder of a central strip 91, and in the plunger of a vertical slot 92. The ejector is constructed with a longitudinal slot 93, so that it may straddle the partition 89 when it is shot rearward to eject a plug from off the bottom of the mold-box. If desired, the rear end of the ejector may be provided with a lubricating-strip 94 upon its upper and lower faces, which are adapted to contain a lubricant which will lessen friction and enable the ejectors to readily reciprocate. This strip also serves to prevent the licorice in the tobacco adhering to the bottom of the mold-box and lower face of the plunger, as these two surfaces are thoroughly lubricated by the said strip in the reciprocation of the ejector.

Having thus described my invention, what I claim, and desire to secure by Letters Patent, is—

1. In a plug-tobacco machine, the combination with a mold-box having vertically-movable sides, a coacting plunger and an ejector, of means for elevating the sides of the mold-box, means for forcing the plunger downward within the mold-box when the sides thereof are elevated, means for lowering the sides of the mold-box, and means for actuating the ejector after the sides of the mold-box have been lowered to eject the plug from the bottom of said box, substantially as set forth.

2. In a plug-tobacco machine, the combination with the mold-box having vertically-movable sides, a feeder for filling said mold-box, a plunger coacting with said mold-box and an ejector, of means for elevating the sides of said mold-box, means for actuating the feeder to fill the mold-box when the sides thereof have been elevated, means for drawing the plunger down into the mold-box after it has been filled, means for lowering the sides of the mold-box after the material therein has been compressed, and means for actuating the ejector to remove the compressed material from the bottom of said mold-box, substantially as set forth.

3. In a plug-tobacco machine, the combination with a mold-box consisting of a bottom and vertically-movable sides, of a feeder to supply said mold-box with material to be compressed, a plunger to compress said material within said mold-box, an ejector for ejecting the compressed material from said mold-box, and means for moving the sides of the mold-box out of the path of movement of the ejector to permit said ejector to move over the bottom of the mold-box, substantially as set forth.

4. In a plug-tobacco machine, the combination with a mold-box having a bottom and sides, said sides being movable to bring the upper edges of two of the same flush with said bottom, a coacting plunger, said plunger being vertically adjustable, whereby the pressure upon the material may be varied, and an ejector for working across the bottom of

the mold-box after the sides have been moved out of the path of movement of the ejector, of means for elevating the sides of the mold-box, means for forcing the plunger downward within the mold-box when the sides thereof are elevated, means for lowering the sides of the mold-box out of the path of movement of the ejector, and means for actuating the ejector after the sides of the mold-box have been lowered to eject the plug from the bottom of said box, substantially as set forth.

5. In a plug-tobacco machine, the combination with a mold-box consisting of a bottom and movable sides, of a feeder to supply said mold-box with material to be compressed, a plunger to compress said material within said box, means for moving the sides, an ejector for ejecting said compressed material from the bottom of said mold-box after the sides have been moved out of the path of movement of the ejector, and a conveyer located at the rear of the machine within the path of movement of the compressed plug to receive said plug after it has been ejected from the mold-box and convey it to a point for further treatment or preparation, substantially as set forth.

6. In a plug-tobacco machine, the combination with a removable mold-box having vertically-movable sides, a removable coacting plunger and an ejector, of means for elevating the sides of the mold-box, means for forcing the plunger downward within the mold-box when the sides thereof are elevated, means for lowering the sides of the mold-box, and means for actuating the ejector after the sides have been lowered to eject the plug from the bottom of said box, substantially as set forth.

7. In a plug-tobacco machine, the combination with a mold-box having vertically-movable sides, a vertically-movable plunger to coöperate with said mold-box, a sliding feeder to supply material to the mold-box and an ejector to eject the compressed material from the mold-box, of an actuating-shaft, a master-wheel fixed thereto having projections thereon, cams fixed to said shaft having crank-pins thereon, links connecting said plunger with said crank-pins on said cams, rods connected to said mold-box and actuated by said cams to raise and lower said mold-box, levers loosely connected to said ejector and feeder and located within the path of movement of said projections carried by the master-wheel for reciprocating said ejector and said feeder, substantially as set forth.

8. In a plug-tobacco machine, the combination with a mold-box, having vertically-movable sides, and its coöperating plunger, a feeder for supplying material to the mold-box, an ejector for ejecting the compressed material, of an operating-shaft, a master-wheel provided with a concentric segmental block and a pin on one face and with a pin projecting from its opposite face, cams mounted on said shaft and having crank-pins thereon, pitmen connecting the plunger to said crank-pins on the cams, bars having their upper ends connected to the movable sides of the mold-box, the lower ends connected to said cams to be reciprocated thereby, levers having their upper ends loosely connected to the feeder and ejector, one of said levers being provided with a curved recess and a straight portion, and with a groove in its side, said straight portion and recess adapted to be engaged by the block, the groove by one of the pins, and the other lever being provided with a straight portion and with a groove, said straight portion and groove adapted to be engaged by the other pin, substantially as set forth.

9. In a plug-tobacco machine, the combination with the compressing devices arranged side by side, of the master-wheels for actuating the compressing devices, a drive-shaft, drive-pinions mounted upon said shaft, a clutch device for locking the pinions to said shaft to rotate therewith, and means for automatically shifting the clutch device for alternately throwing into and out of gear the master-wheels, substantially as set forth.

10. In a plug-tobacco machine, the combination with a mold-box having vertically-movable sides, a coacting plunger and an ejector, of means for elevating the sides of the mold-box, means for forcing the plunger downward within the mold-box when its sides are elevated, means for lowering the sides of the mold-box, means for actuating the ejector after the sides of the mold-box have been lowered to eject the plug from the bottom of said box, and a lubricator actuated by the ejector for lubricating the opposing faces of the mold-box bottom and plunger, substantially as set forth.

In testimony whereof I have hereunto set my hand in presence of two subscribing witnesses.

GEORGE T. LESTER.

Witnesses:
H. B. WILLSON,
BENJ. G. COWL.

Aug. 15, 1950

G. T. LESTER, SR
FURNACE FOR BURNING COMMINUTED FUEL,
INCLUDING TANGENTIAL AIR FEED

2,518,800

Filed July 14, 1948

3 Sheets—Sheet 1

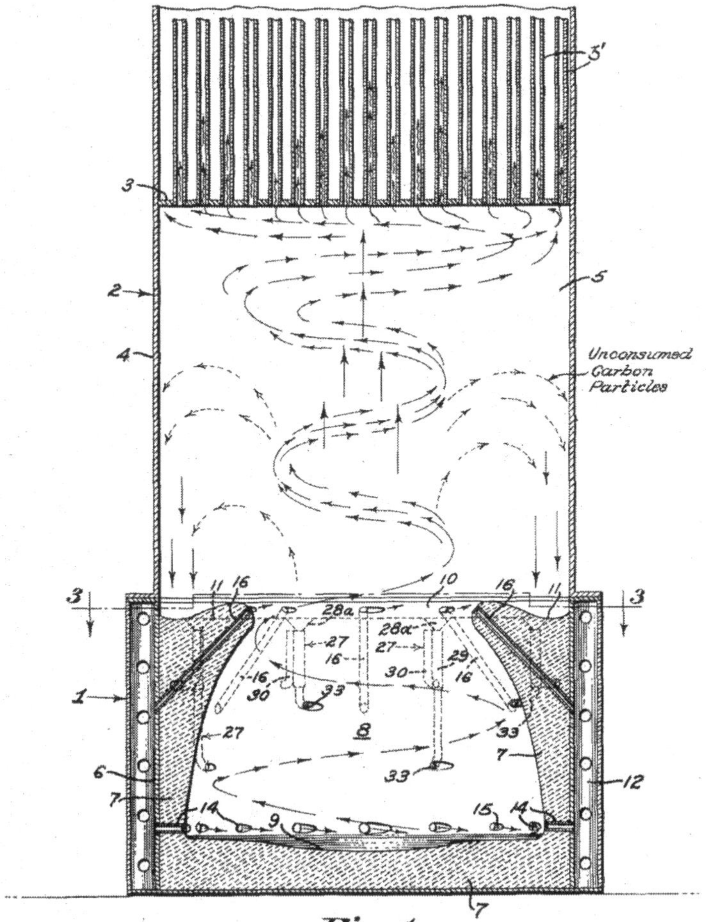

Fig. 1

Inventor
GEORGE T. LESTER, SR.

By Mason, Fenwick & Lawrence
Attorneys

Aug. 15, 1950 G. T. LESTER, SR 2,518,800
FURNACE FOR BURNING COMMINUTED FUEL, INCLUDING TANGENTIAL AIR FEED
Filed July 14, 1948 3 Sheets-Sheet 2

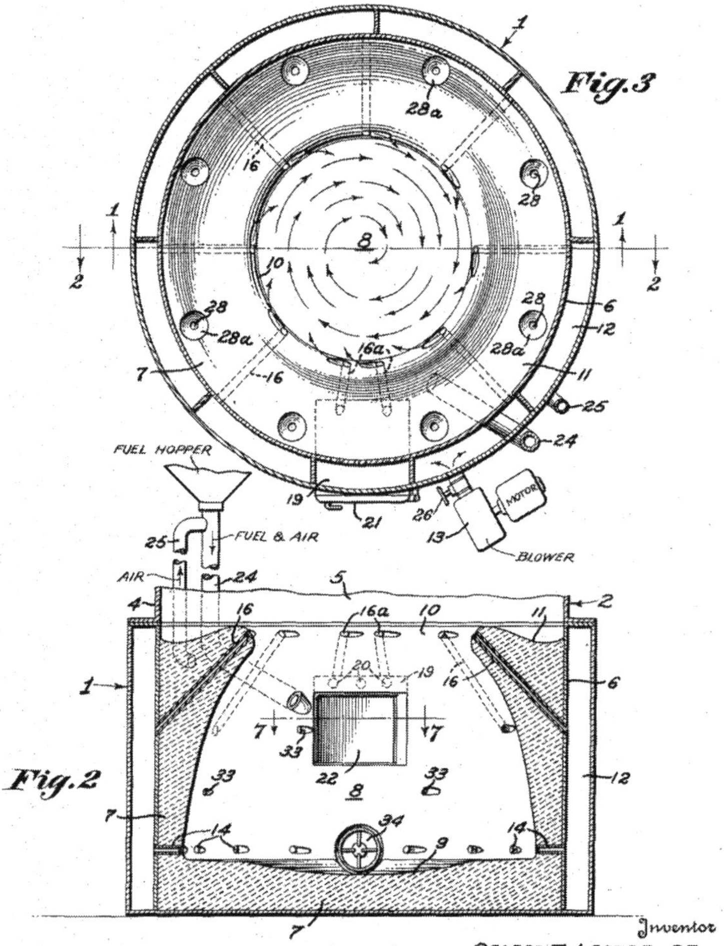

Inventor
GEORGE T. LESTER, SR.

By Mason, Fenwick & Lawrence
Attorneys

Aug. 15, 1950 G. T. LESTER, SR **2,518,800**

FURNACE FOR BURNING COMMINUTED FUEL, INCLUDING TANGENTIAL AIR FEED

Filed July 14, 1948 3 Sheets-Sheet 3

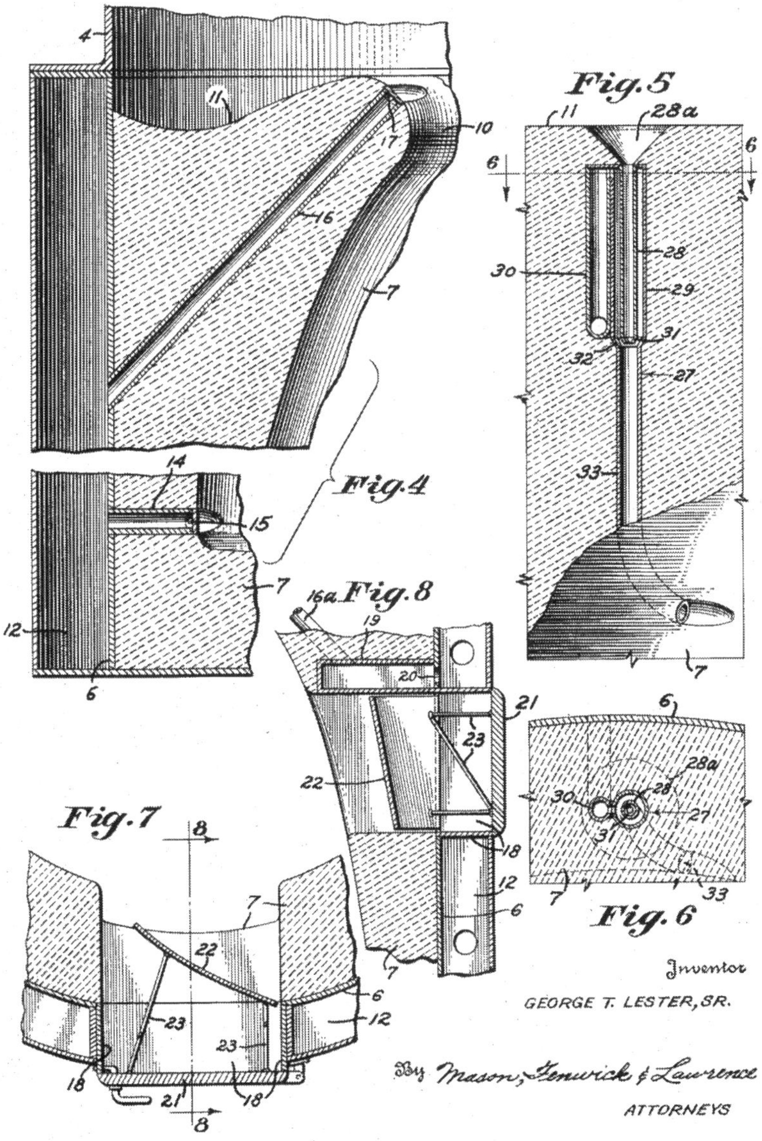

Inventor

GEORGE T. LESTER, SR.

By Mason, Fenwick & Lawrence

ATTORNEYS

Patented Aug. 15, 1950

2,518,800

UNITED STATES PATENT OFFICE

2,518,800

FURNACE FOR BURNING COMMINUTED FUEL, INCLUDING TANGENTIAL AIR FEED

George T. Lester, Sr., Martinsville, Va.

Application July 14, 1948, Serial No. 38,634

9 Claims. (Cl. 110—28)

This invention relates to a furnace for efficiently producing smokeless combustion of comminuted fuel.

One of the objects of the invention is to provide a means for generating heat from comminuted fuel such as sawdust, pulverized coal, etc., by burning the fuel in a combustion chamber in a whirling atmosphere continuously supplied, causing the products of combustion to expand into a chamber more capacious than the combustion chamber and of larger diameter, the combustion products still whirling with sufficient velocity to throw unconsumed particles to the periphery of the expansion chamber, thereby creating a clarified central column of combustion gases which flows to the heat exchanger, usually a boiler, and ultimately to the stack, and creating a downward drift of the atmosphere of the expansion chamber adjacent the periphery thereof and its return to the combustion chamber with the centrifugally displaced unconsumed fuel particles, so that the combustion of said particles can be completed.

Another object of the invention is to provide, in a furnace of the type which has a combustion chamber and a superposed expansion chamber of greater capacity and diameter than the combustion chamber, with a restricted mouth between said chambers, in which fuel is burned in said combustion chamber in a whirling atmosphere produced by the admission of air under pressure in a circumferential direction, and in which the whirling products of combustion expand within the expansion chamber, whereby unconsumed particles are thrown to the periphery of said chamber, but by virtue of the expansion are under less pressure than that in the combustion chamber, passages communicating with the peripheral portion of said expansion chamber and with said combustion chamber and means for drawing the centrifugally displaced unconsumed particles through said passages into said combustion chamber against the superior pressure existing in said combustion chamber.

A further object of the invention is to provide a furnace of the type described, having a refractory lining in the combustion chamber intersected by circumferential series of air inlet tubes in zones adjacent the bottom, top, and intermediately, whereby the lining is sufficiently cooled to prevent it from fusing, and the entering air correspondingly preheated.

Other objects of the invention will appear as the following description of a preferred and practical embodiment thereof proceeds.

In the drawings which accompany and form a part of the specification:

Figure 1 is a vertical section through a furnace and the associated end of a vertical boiler, embodying the principles of the invention, taken along the line 1—1 of Figure 3, viewed in the direction of the inner arrows;

Figure 2 is a similar view of the furnace on the same section line, viewed in the direction of the outer arrows;

Figure 3 is a cross-section taken along the line 3—3 of Figure 1;

Figure 4 is a fragmentary detail in vertical section of a portion of the refractory lining of the combustion chamber, showing an upper and lower tuyère;

Figure 5 is a fragmentary detail in vertical section through a portion of the refractory lining showing one of the injectors;

Figure 6 is a cross-section taken along the line 6—6 of Figure 5;

Figure 7 is a horizontal section through the door opening showing the door and adjacent environment, taken along the line 7—7 of Figure 2;

Figure 8 is a vertical section taken along the line 8—8 of Figure 7.

Referring now in detail to the description of the invention as illustrated, the numeral 1 represents a cylindrical furnace upon which a tubular boiler 2 is mounted coaxially of the furnace. The crown sheet 3 of the boiler is some distance within the boiler shell 4, the space 5 within the shell and below the crown sheet being hereinafter referred to as the expansion chamber.

The furnace comprises a metal casing 6, provided on the inside both on the bottom and sides, with a refractory lining 7, which lining defines a combustion chamber 8, the bottom of which preferably has a slightly concave depression in the middle, as indicated at 9, and the sides of which converge upwardly, forming a somewhat retricted mouth 10, communicating with the expansion chamber, and also defining an annular mantel 11, surrounding the mouth and forming the bottom of the expansion chamber.

The casing 6 is provided with an air jacket 12 surrounding the combustion chamber, supplied with air under some pressure by a blower 13, controlled by a valve 26. A pressure of one-half pound may be mentioned as a practical working pressure, but this may be varied, within the invention, according to the conditions of use. The jacket 12 is the reservoir for all the air supplied to the combustion chamber, including that which comes in as a vehicle for the fuel. The jacket 12 is preferably coextensive with the height of the furnace, in view of its cooling effect upon the sides of the refractory lining 7.

A circumferential series of uniformly spaced tuyères 14 open into the combustion chamber in a zone adjacent the bottom. These communicate with the jacket 12, extend radially through the refractory lining, terminate as close as possible to the inner surface of said lining, and are closed at their inner ends except for a single lateral hole 15. The holes of all the tuyères 14 face in the same circumferential direction, serving as nozzles to organize a whirling atmosphere within the combustion chamber.

Another circumferential series of tuyères 16 open into the combustion chamber in the zone of the mouth 10, communicating with the jacket 12, passing through the refractory lining in an upwardly inclined position, and terminating in the relatively thin lip of refractory material that bounds the circumference of the mouth. These tuyères likewise are closed at the ends, except for the single lateral holes 17 which face in the same direction as the holes in the lower series of tuyères. The function of the tuyères 16 is to augment the whirling movement of the gaseous atmosphere of the combustion chamber, as well as to provide additional air for combustion. They also cool the upper part of the refractory lining through which they extend, and give it structural support.

The casing 6 is provided with a rectangular metal frame 18, at a point intermediate its height, defining a door opening which gives access to the interior of the combustion chamber for kindling a fire, and also serving as a manhole. The frame 18 bridges the jacket space, being welded or otherwise secured to the inner and outer jacket walls in an airtight manner all around. The sides and bottom members of the frame 18 terminate flush with the inner and outer jacket walls, but the top member 19 projects inwardly for a distance equal to the thickness of the refractory lining so as to support the overlying refractory material. The top frame member 19 is hollow and has holes 20 therethrough, which communicate with the air jacket 12, and the drawings show that two of the tuyères of the upper series 16a are welded to the member 19, communicating with said jacket through the interior of said member. Air passing through said tuyères from the jacket 12 cools the member 19 as well as the refractory material through which the tuyères 16a extend. The refractory lining 7 has an opening therethrough substantially congruent with the door opening defined by the frame 18.

A door 21 hinged to the outer wall of the air jacket at the approach side of the door opening, with respect to the direction of circumferential travel of the gases within the combustion chamber, and closes against said outer wall. Said door carries an inclined baffle 22, spaced therefrom and supported by rods 23. Said baffle starts substantially flush with the inner wall of the jacket 12, at the hinged side of the door, and terminates substantially flush with the inner surface of the refractory lining at the opposite side. The main object of the baffle is to streamline the whirling gases passing the door opening, so that they will not strike abruptly the refractory lining adjacent the free side of the door and create turbulence which would interrupt the orderly unidirectional circumferential swirl of said gases. Its other object is to protect the door from becoming unduly heated. The aggregate cross-sectional area of the rods 23 is the minimum required for their necessary supporting strength, and presents the minimum thermally conductive path from baffle to door.

Comminuted fuel is supplied gravitationally through a pipe 24, which passes through the casing 6 and the refractory lining 7, intersecting the air jacket 12. The inner end of this pipe opens into the combustion chamber adjacent the approach side of the door opening and is inclined toward the baffle at such an angle that the resultant of gravity and the circumferential swirl of the gaseous atmosphere of the combustion chamber causes the entering fuel to spiral downwardly toward the concave middle of the refractory bottom 7. A pipe 25 taps the jacket 12 and enters the fuel pipe 24 at some distance from the furnace, the gravitational flow of fuel toward the combustion chamber being assisted by air at jacket pressure. The flow of this air past the baffle cools the baffle.

In starting a cold furnace, the fire can be most conveniently kindled, assuming that the fuel is sawdust, by throwing a piece of lighted oil-soaked waste through the door opening onto the floor of the combustion chamber near the middle. The air valve 26 is then opened to admit air to the jacket 12, thus organizing the whirling atmosphere within the combustion chamber. The fuel is then admitted, which deposits upon the burning waste and is ignited. At first, a mass of fuel may accumulate in the depression 9, burning from the top, but as the heat intensifies, most of the fuel is burned in suspension before it reaches the bottom of the furnace, any pile that may have previously accumulated being progressively burned away by attrition. When the furnace is in full combustion, the combustion chamber is filled with whirling flame so intense that the surface of the refractory lining is heated to white incandescence, at which temperature the best known lining material would melt if it were not for the distributed cooling of the same effected by the proximity of the air jacket 12, the air passing through the lower and upper series of tuyères 14 and 16, the air admitted with the fuel, and air flowing through passages in an intermediate zone of said refractory lining, presently to be described.

The flaming products of combustion issue from the mouth 10 under the combined forces of convection, thermal expansion and displacement by the air entering the combustion chamber, and they rise in the form of a whirling column which expands in the expansion chamber 5, the latter being of greater cubic capacity than the combustion chamber. In a practical embodiment of the invention now in successful operation, the expansion chamber has eight times the volume of the combustion chamber. Expansion reduces the upward velocity of the ascending column of combustion products, giving time for the substantial completion of combustion in the expansion chamber so that the flames die out before reaching the crown sheet, the latter being thus protected from excessive heating with the attendant risk of producing a steam pocket at the adjacent end of the boiler, forcing the water back and leaving dry boiler surface to be overheated by the intensely hot flames. The open ends of the boiler tubes 3' in the crown sheet 3 are, as is customary, uniformly distributed throughout the area of the crown sheet, resulting in a uniform discharge of the combustion products of the furnace throughout the area of the crown sheet, producing the symmetrical vortex indicated by the arrows in Figure 1.

The combustion products in the expansion chamber are, however, interspersed with a constituent of incompletely consumed fuel particles which ordinarily would be drawn through the boiler tubes and appear at the top of the stack as smoke, representing wasted fuel, besides, fouling the boiler tubes and depositing a heat insulating carbon film on the interior surfaces of the tubes, thus decreasing the efficiency of the boiler. These unconsumed particles are centrifugally thrown toward the periphery of the expansion chamber, clarifying the central column of gases rising through said chamber. The heavier particles strike the inner surface of the shell 4 and, their motion being arrested, they drop upon the mantel 11. The lighter particles circulate suspended in a peripheral zone of combustion gases outside of the central clarified column. The diminution in the velocity of ascent of the combustion products in the expansion chamber gives time for the complete centrifugal separation of the unconsumed fuel particles before the combustion gases enter the boiler.

The present invention provides for the return of these unconsumed particles to the combustion chamber to be burned, and the procedure is to withdraw them from a region of relatively less pressure and to introduce them into a region of relatively greater pressure. This is done in the following manner.

A series of injectors 27 is provided, embedded in the refractory lining 7 in alternate arrangement with respect to most of the tuyères 16. Each injector, as shown, consists of a vertically positioned carbon tube 28, having its upper end opening in the face of the mantel 11 near its outer periphery at the bottom of a funnel shaped depression 28a, formed in said mantel. Said carbon tube is surrounded by a larger tube 29, forming an annular air conduit thereabout. At the side of the annular air conduit and axially parallel thereto is an air pipe 30, communicating with said annular conduit near the top and communicating at its lower end with the air jacket 12. The lower ends of the carbon tube 28 and the surrounding tube 29, in the same zone, are inwardly beveled to form inner and outer nozzles 31 and 32. Air entering the air pipe 30 under pressure from the air jacket 12 issues from the nozzle 32, creating suction at the nozzle 31. This induces a down drift of the atmosphere of the expansion chamber in the peripheral region, drawing it back into the combustion chamber together with the displaced unconsumed fuel particles that it contains. The carbon tube and the annular conduit 29 terminate in a common tail pipe 33, which extends through the refractory lining 7 and opens tangentially in its inner surface in the same direction as the holes in the tuyères. The tail pipe 33 passes combustion gases from the expansion chamber mixed with air from the air jacket, said air providing the necessary oxygen for burning the unconsumed particles which are spontaneously ignited at the point at which they enter the intensely hot combustion chamber.

The mantel 11 slopes downward toward its outer periphery so as to cause such particles which may lodge on said mantel and are swept about by the whirling gases, to gravitate outwardly and be caught in the funnel shaped depressions and drawn through the injector.

The injectors extend longitudinally through the refractory lining for the major portion of their length to present as great a surface as possible in heat exchanging contact with the refractory material for cooling the latter, and the tail pipes of alternate injectors extend to a lower level than the tail pipes of the remaining injectors, so that they open into the combustion chamber in separate intermediate zones at different levels, whereby they more or less uniformly distribute their cooling function throughout the mass of the refractory lining between the zones of the lower and upper tuyères. All of the air entering the combustion chamber through the tuyères, injectors, and fuel pipe passes through the heated refractory lining and is preheated.

The down drift in the peripheral region of the expansion chamber atmosphere is inherently more feeble than the forces which tend to lift the central column of clarified combustion gases toward the crown sheet of the boiler. Therefore, it is not felt in the upper regions of the expansion chamber, so that above the down drift the column of clarified combustion gases is free to expand outwardly as well as upwardly so that it extends to the shell 4 and thus becomes uniformly distributed throughout the entire area of the crown sheet and through all the tubes of the boiler, while the combustion gases within the expansion chamber will have become centrifugally purged of all unconsumed particles by the time they reach the height at which they are unaffected by the down drift.

It will be understood that all of the air-admitting instrumentalities which pass through the refractory lining 7 are directly supported by the casing 6 and in turn lend support to said lining.

In a furnace constructed according to the teachings of the invention as herein disclosed, combustion is so complete that when the furnace is in normal operation, no smoke can be detected at the mouth of the stack. Neither is it necessary to remove any ashes over long periods of operation, since the noncombustible residue has the form of a light fly ash which is discharged from the stack suspended in the effluent gases. With certain types of fuel, a fused clinker may form in the bottom of the combustion chamber, and a clinker door 34 is provided at the base of the furnace, closing an opening to the combustion chamber through which the clinker may from time to time be withdrawn. In general, however, this door is useful to admit air for quick cooling of the furnace when this becomes necessary, for making repairs, etc.

While I have in the above disclosure described what I believe to be a preferred and practical embodiment of the invention, it will be understood by those skilled in the art that the specific details of the construction and arrangement of parts, as shown, are by way of example and not to be construed as limiting the scope of the invention.

What I claim as my invention is:

1. In furnace construction, means defining coaxial combustion and expansion chambers, the expansion chamber being above said combustion chamber and of larger diameter and capacity than said combustion chamber, said chambers communicating by way of a constricted central mouth which defines an upwardly facing annular mantel constituting the bottom of said expansion chamber, means for admitting comminuted fuel

to said combustion chamber, means for admitting air at the periphery of said combustion chamber tangentially, producing a whirling atmosphere in said combustion chamber which persists in the column of combustion products that discharges through said mouth and expands in said expansion chamber, whereby unconsumed fuel particles are centrifugally thrown to a peripheral zone of said expansion chamber above said mantel, passage means opening in said mantel leading to said combustion chamber, and means for withdrawing said centrifugally displaced unconsumed particles from said peripheral zone and returning them to said combustion chamber through said passages.

2. In furnace construction, means defining coaxial combustion and expansion chambers, the expansion chamber being above said combustion chamber and of larger diameter and capacity than said combustion chamber, said chambers communicating by way of a constricted central mouth which defines an upwardly facing annular mantel constituting the bottom of said expansion chamber, means for admitting comminuted fuel to said combustion chamber, means for admitting air at the periphery of said combustion chamber tangentially, producing a whirling atmosphere in said combustion chamber which persists in the column of combustion products that discharges through said mouth and expands in said expansion chamber, whereby unconsumed fuel particles are centrifugally thrown to a peripheral zone of said expansion chamber above said mantel, and injector means including passages opening in said mantel and leading to said combustion chamber for withdrawing said centrifugally displaced unconsumed particles from said peripheral zone and returning them to said combustion chamber through said passages.

3. In furnace construction, means defining coaxial combustion and expansion chambers, the expansion chamber being above said combustion chamber and of larger diameter and capacity than said combustion chamber, said chambers directly communicating by way of a central constricted mouth which defines an upwardly facing annular mantel constituting the bottom of said expansion chamber, a transverse sheet forming the end of said expansion chamber opposite said mouth, having substantially throughout its entirety a plurality of substantially uniformly distributed openings through which the combustion gases from said expansion chamber discharge, means for admitting comminuted fuel to said combustion chamber, means for admitting air at the periphery of said combustion chamber tangentially, producing a whirling atmosphere in said combustion chamber which persists in the column of combustion products that discharges through said mouth and expands in said expansion chamber, whereby unconsumed fuel particles are centrifugally thrown to a peripheral zone of said expansion chamber above said mantel, and injectors including passages opening in said mantel leading to said combustion chamber, for withdrawing said centrifugally displaced unconsumed particles from said peripheral zone and returning them to said combustion chamber.

4. In furnace construction, a combustion chamber unit comprising a cylindrical metal casing having a surrounding air jacket and means for supplying air under pressure to said jacket, an expansion chamber unit comprising a shell coaxial with said combustion chamber unit and resting thereupon having a transverse sheet at some distance from the lower end of the shell, the space within said shell below said sheet constituting an expansion chamber, said sheet being provided substantially throughout its entirety with a plurality of substantially uniformly distributed openings for the discharge of combustion gases said casing having a refractory lining with upwardly convergent sides defining a combustion chamber having a constricted mouth and forming an annular mantel surrounding said mouth constituting the bottom of said expansion chamber, the latter being of greater capacity than said combustion chamber, a fuel pipe for feeding pulverized fuel to said combustion chamber, a circumferential series of tuyères from said jacket extending through said refractory lining, opening tangentially into said combustion chamber for producing a whirling atmosphere therein which persists in the column of combustion products that discharges through said mouth toward said sheet and expands in said expansion chamber, whereby unconsumed fuel particles are thrown to a peripheral zone of said expansion chamber above said mantel, and a circumferential series of injectors, each including an air tube from said jacket opening into said combustion chamber, and a carbon tube having its upper end opening in said mantel, extending into said air tube axially thereof and terminating therewithin, whereby the flow of air under pressure from said jacket past said carbon tube withdraws said centrifugally displaced unconsumed particles from said peripheral zone, returning them to said combustion chamber.

5. In furnace construction, a combustion chamber unit adapted to be installed beneath an expansion chamber of greater diameter and capacity than the combustion chamber and having a discharge at the end remote from said unit, said unit comprising a cylindrical casing having a jacketed space thereabout extending substantially the height of the casing and supplied by air under pressure, a refractory lining within said casing including bottom and side walls, the latter converging in an upward direction defining a constricted mouth and a mantel surrounding the mouth, said lining defining a combustion chamber, a circumferential series of tuyères entering said combustion chamber through said lining near the bottom, a circumferential series of upwardly and inwardly directed tuyères extending through said lining, entering said combustion chamber adjacent said mouth, the tuyères of both series opening tangentially in the same direction, a circumferential series of injectors extending through said lining entering said combustion chamber in a zone between said series of tuyères, said injectors each including a carbon tube having its upper end opening in said mantel, and an air tube into which the lower end of said carbon tube extends and opens, whereby the flow of air through said air tube creates downward flow through said carbon tube, said tuyères of both series and the air tubes of said injectors being supported by said casing and communicating with said jacket.

6. Furnace construction as claimed in claim 5, including a fuel pipe for feeding pulverized fuel to said combustion chamber and a connection establishing communication between said jacket and said fuel pipe.

7. Furnace construction as claimed in claim 6, said mantel sloping downwardly toward its outer periphery, and the carbon tubes of said injectors opening into said mantel near its outer periphery.

8. Furnace construction as claimed in claim 6, said injectors opening into said combustion chamber at different levels.

9. In a furnace of that type comprising a combustion chamber for burning comminuted fuel including a metal casing having a refractory lining, to which combustion chamber air for combustion is admitted tangentially setting up a whirling atmosphere within said combustion chamber, said combustion chamber having a door opening intermediate its height through said casing and refractory lining, a door hinged to said casing on the approach side of said opening with reference to the direction of said whirling atmosphere, said door closing against said casing, an inclined baffle carried by said door in spaced relation thereto extending from the outer face of said lining on the approach side of said opening to the inner face of said lining on the opposite side of said opening, and a fuel pipe entering said combustion chamber adjacent the approach side of said door opening having its inner end inclined toward said baffle, for admitting fuel in a vehicle of air under pressure whereby the air cools said baffle.

GEORGE T. LESTER, Sr.

REFERENCES CITED

The following references are of record in the file of this patent:

UNITED STATES PATENTS

Number	Name	Date
1,112,463	Meikle	Oct. 6, 1914
1,657,698	Schutz	Jan. 31, 1928
1,817,150	Hvoslef	Aug. 4, 1931
1,918,397	Jezler	July 18, 1933
1,943,949	Coghlan et al.	Jan. 16, 1934
1,967,883	Hofmann	July 24, 1934
1,969,371	Hawley	Aug. 7, 1934
2,424,765	McCollum	July 29, 1947

Acknowledgements

When a man reaches his seventh decade of life, he naturally thinks of his past and accomplishments. The future looms large. Thoughts of mortality and the legacy one leaves behind are foremost in one's mind. Such I believe was the case for George W. Lester II in the spring of 2009 when he approached me about working on a project about his family especially his father George Tilden "Cap'n Til" Lester. This work is the product of that initial contact and many hours of research, interviews, and following the path of the Lester Family of Henry County, Virginia, from the founding of this nation through the continued contribution of the Lester name in the business and philanthropic worlds.

This work came from interviews with many persons including the aforementioned George W. Lester II, Morton Lester and Ralph C. Lester and George Oakley. Also, consulted were John Redd Smith and Douglas Stegall. Special thanks to Carol Lovell for bringing in the video made by the late Martinsville Police Officer Scott Witherow in 1987 of the Liberty Heights Swimming Pool as demolition occurred.

The staff of the Bassett Historical Center continued to support this work as it has for my other ten books at this writing. Thanks to Patricia Ross, Anne Copeland, Sam Eanes, and Cindy Headen at that facility.

The best story relating to those who assisted with this book belongs to Linda Stanley of the Franklin County Historical Society. Linda announced to me that she once wore "Mrs. Lester's wedding dress" after she returned from South Carolina where she married Jay Stanley in the mid 1960s. Linda lived on Starling Avenue while working for Lester Brothers in Martinsville with Mrs. Ethel Lester Overton. When apprised of the recent nuptials, Mrs. Overton felt that a proper wedding portrait was required and walked across Starling Avenue to the "Wedding Cake" house and returned with a beautiful dress imported from China. See the result of this marriage of Stanleys and Lester wedding dress.

The experience of writing this book was at once educational learning more about Henry County history than I could ever hope to know and entertaining spending time with the many Lesters especially Ralph C. and George W. Lester II, who made this one of the best experiences of my writing life.

-- Tom Perry, July 2009 and 2012, Kernersville, North Carolina.

Bibliography

Manuscript Collections
    Franklin County Virginia Historical Society
        Waid File
        Menefee File
        Franklin County Post Offices over the Years
    Bassett Historical Center
        Connolly, J. M. Lester Family, Dallas, Texas
        Grady Garrett Collection, Volume 53 Lee-Letcher
        Payne, Ronald W., History of Koehler.
        Winn, William. Tragedy on Fayette Street.
        Family Files on Lesters, Waids, Turner, Shelton,
        Topical Files on the Dick and Willie Railroad, Norfolk and
        Southern Railroad, Liberty Heights, Koehler,
    George W. Lester II
        Photo album by Elizabeth Lester Walsh

Library of Virginia http://www.lva.virginia.gov
    Pension Records of G. W. Lester and W. A. Lester
    WPA Files on Waid and Henry Clay Lester houses

Virginia Tech
    Compiled Service Records of G. W. Lester John C. Lester and W. A. Lester

U. S. Census 1830 and 1840: Free Inhabitants
U. S. Census 1850: Free Inhabitants, Slave and Agricultural Schedules
U. S. Census 1860: Free Inhabitants, Slave and Agricultural Schedules
U. S. Census 1870: Inhabitants and Agricultural Schedules

Newspapers articles on the Lesters from the Martinsville Bulletin, Henry Bulletin, Henry Herald Memorial Edition 1899; July 1920; May 29, 1949; November 15, 1950; November 24, 1950; November 10, 1957; July 6, 1960; November 23, 1969; March 21, 1973; February 14, 1975; April 27, 1975; June 15, 1975; June 13, 1976; March 18, 1979; May 7, 1979; June 13, 1979; August 23, 1981; October 13, 1981; December 16, 1981; April 18, 1982; May 15, 1983; January 10, 1984; February 6, 1987; June 24, 1990; January 6, 1991;

October 1, 1993; January 14, 1996; June 2, 1996; October 19, 1999; November 15, 1999; June 5, 2001; February 5, 2002; May 31, 2002; August 4, 2002; March 26, 2006; November 22, 2006; November 21, 2007; November 29, 2007; February 27, 2008; May 9, 2008, on the Lanier Farm; October 19, 2008 on Shady Grove; April 26, 2009

Richmond Times Dispatch
    August 23, 1981; February 27, 2008
Roanoke Times
    September 7, 2007, Sports Complex Opens at Waid Park

Interviews
    George W. Lester II, Ralph C. Lester, Carol Lovell, George D. Oakley, Julia Lester Oakley (Transcribed), John Redd Smith

Books
Cleal, Dorothy and Herbert, Hiram H. Foresight, Founders and Fortitude
Driver, Robert J. Tenth Virginia Cavalry, H. E. Howard, Lynchburg, VA. 1985.
Honeywell, Mary Waid. The Waid Family of Franklin County Virginia. Albion, Michigan, 1991.
Jacobs, E. B. History of Roanoke City, 1912.
Lester, Ralph C. Lester Family Book, Martinsville 1996.
Lester, Ralph C. Magnet: A Commentary. Nashville TN, 2007.
Menefee, Josephine T. History of Pleasant Hill and its occupants 1804-1944.
Morris, Whit. The First Tunstalls in Virginia, San Antonio, 1950.
Perry, Thomas D. J. E. B. Stuart's Birthplace: The History of the Laurel Hill Farm. Ararat VA. 2007
Perry, Thomas D. The Free State of Patrick: Patrick County Virginia in the Civil War, Ararat VA. 2007
Salmon, John S. Franklin County Virginia 1786-1986: A Bicentennial History, Rocky Mount, VA, 1993.
Sponangle, William C., Biographies of Southwestern Virginians, Volume One.
Sublett, Charles W. 57th Virginia Infantry, 1985. H. E. Howard, Lynchburg, VA.
Tyler, Lyon G. Men of Mark in Virginia Volume IV.
Sign of the Times, Volume 126 Number 6, Danville, VA, June 1958.

Made in the USA
Columbia, SC
29 October 2020